SOCIAL PROBLEMS IN POPULAR CULTURE

R.J. Maratea

Brian Monahan

First published in Great Britain in 2016 by

Policy Press
University of Bristol
1-9 Old Park Hill
Bristol BS2 8BB
UK
t: +44 (0)117 954 5940
e: pp-info@bristol.ac.uk
www.policypress.co.uk

North American office:
Policy Press
c/o The University of Chicago Press
1427 East 60th Street
Chicago, IL 60637, USA
t: +1 773 702 7700
f: +1 773-702-9756
e:sales@press.uchicago.edu
www.press.uchicago.edu

© Policy Press 2016

British Library Cataloguing in Publication Data
A catalogue record for this book is available from the British Library.

Library of Congress Cataloging-in-Publication Data
A catalog record for this book has been requested.

ISBN 978-1-4473-2158-3 paperback
ISBN 978-1-4473-2157-6 hardcover
ISBN 978-1-4473-2160-6 ePub
ISBN 978-1-4473-2161-3 Mobi
ISBN 978-1-4473-2159-0 ePdf

The right of R.J. Maratea and Brian Monahan to be identified as authors of this work has been asserted by them in accordance with the 1988 Copyright, Designs and Patents Act.

Cover design by Andrew Corbett
Front cover: image kindly supplied by picturetank

For Joel Best

Table of contents

Notes on authors

R.J. Maratea is Visiting Assistant Professor of Criminal Justice at Seton Hall University. His research interests include capital punishment and the implications of mass communication as they pertain to the construction of cultural and political realities, institutionalized inequality, deviant and criminal identities, and the institutionalization of social control. He is the author of *The politics of the internet: Political claims-making and its affect on modern political activism* (published by Lexington, 2014), and co-editor (with David P. Keys) of *Race and the death penalty: The legacy of McCleskey v. Kemp* (published by Lynne Rienner, 2016). His work has also appeared in journals such as *Social Problems, Symbolic Interaction, Journal of the History of the Behavioral Sciences, Deviant Behavior, Qualitative Sociology Review, Sexualities*, and *Sociology Compass*.

Brian Monahan is Associate Professor of Sociology and Criminal Justice at Marywood University. His scholarly interests include the ways in which mass media and public officials create and spread shared meanings about crime, deviance, and social problems. He is the author of *The shock of the news: Media coverage and the making of 9/11* (published by NYU, 2010) and his work has appeared in a variety of edited volumes and journals such as *Symbolic Interaction, Deviant Behavior*, and *Journal of Contemporary Ethnography*.

Acknowledgements

This book would not have been possible without the guidance and mentorship of some amazing scholars to whom both authors owe far more than they can express with a simple acknowledgement: Joel Best and David Altheide have each shaped our intellectual development and imparted upon us unique and valued scholarly perspectives. We thank each of you for your contributions and help in making this project a reality. Additional thanks go to Tammy Anderson, Aaron Kupchik, David Keys, John Hepburn, John Johnson, Giancarlo Panagia, Rebecca Tiger, and the debonair Terry Lilley for providing input, feedback, resources, and mentorship along the way. We are also grateful to the anonymous reviewers who provided invaluable feedback that made the manuscript better in so many ways.

The staff at Policy Press also deserve recognition for their tremendous support and professionalism. In particular, Rebecca Tomlinson, Victoria Pittman, and Emily Watt have all provided us with the flexibility and encouragement to shape and reshape the book's thesis, and allow us to produce a text we are excited to share with our colleagues and students. Thank you for allowing us to stay true to ourselves as scholars.

Finally, we could not have reached this point without the support of our families, friends, and an extraordinary group of professional colleagues and students who perpetually reinvigorate our desire to teach and learn. R.J. wishes to thank his family, as well as John Sullivan, Brian Owin, Debra D'Agostino, Jason Ordini, Jamie Longazel, Phil Kavanaugh, Carlos Posadas, Dana Greene, Dulcinea Lara, and Robert Duran. Brian thanks his wife, Lauren, and their children – Ashlyn, Colin, Jason, and Keaton – for the love and laughter they provide each and every day.

ONE

Introduction

Franklin D. Roosevelt famously claimed in 1933, "The only thing we have to fear is fear itself." These days it often seems like there are so many sources of harm in the world that "fear itself" is the least of our concerns. National and local news reports are littered with statistics, images, and tragic tales about one social ill or another every single day. Public statements from politicians offer grave depictions of a world in crisis. Those who watch daytime talk shows are likely to have noticed the steady stream of traumatized victims sharing their stories to raise awareness about particular social concerns. Some readers may even participate in the larger responses to particular social problems by donating money to charity or taking physical action during protest rallies, marches, or even by dumping a bucket of ice water over their heads and sharing the video with their social network. Others engage with social problems in much different and considerably more personal ways by directly experiencing them (eg drug or alcohol addiction, eating disorders, student loan debt and so on). The point here is that we all confront social problems in more ways than we might realize simply by going about our daily routines.

Popular culture, too, is a topic with which you are no doubt well acquainted. Most everyone in modern society actively engages with popular culture in some capacity. Simple activities such as watching television, downloading music, going to the movies, playing video games, reading a book, wearing clothes, and interacting on social media are all ways of participating in popular culture. From a sociological perspective, however, it can be challenging to figure out how all of these things directly influence our individual and collective understanding of the world around us. Pop culture, after all, encompasses all of the things people experience in everyday mass culture and directly influences how we respond to the issues and events that we all regularly confront in public life. The truth is popular culture serves as a lens for most everything that happens in the social world. Throughout this book we will attempt to show how and why popular culture is not simply the latest Taylor Swift song or a Kim Kardashian sex tape, but rather a mechanism of social power deeply immersed in the fabric of our global society. More specifically, popular culture is a vehicle for generating and communicating meanings and messages that influence how individuals craft their identities, interact with others, and understand social issues. It can also promote conformity and solidarity, while at the same time stimulating social change. You may recall that following the 9/11 terrorist attacks that popular culture was roundly praised as a key force in the nation's recovery. President George W. Bush implored Americans to buy things and take vacations; and the return of National Football League games was cited as a crucial ingredient in the country's collective efforts to "return to normal". Yet pop culture can also operate as a divisive force, such as when President Obama was criticized for glorifying criminal behavior when he invited the rap artist Common to perform in a poetry reading at the White House in 2011. The key is to understand that popular culture exerts considerable authority over how we interpret the social world, even if it is not always evident how and why movies, television, advertising, fashion, and countless other cultural elements actually wield such influence.

A central theme running through this book is that popular culture helps to direct us to look at and respond in a variety of ways to social problems like racial inequality, sexism, climate change, and human rights violations. These days most people need look no further for evidence of this fact than scrolling through their personal social media feeds or using popular apps; doing so will likely reveal messages and links related to friends' concerns, invitations to participate in online or real-world protests, requests to display certain colors or symbols in support of particular causes, and request to share information about social problems with other people in your network. Similarly, television shows, movies, and popular music are rife with messages about all sorts of social issues like drug abuse, bullying, eating disorders, gender norms, violence, poverty, war, and police corruption. Sometimes these messages are viewed positively in the fight to cure a social problem. During the 1970s, for example, *All in the Family's* iconic Archie Bunker curmudgeonly showed television audiences the insidious nature of racism and sexism. More recently, shows like *Glee* have helped normalize homosexual and transgender sexual orientations that were historically viewed as deviant by a large portion of the population (and continue to be in many parts of the world). At other times, popular culture is blamed as the cause of social ills, such as when films or musicians are vilified for promoting violence or new technologies are depicted as causing new problems, such as recent fears that the dating app *Tinder* is spawning a "dating apocalypse" by prompting young men and women to only value superficial relationships and meaningless sex (see Sales, 2015).

Admittedly, it would be difficult to convince some readers that casual sex is a social problem, but this is not really the point. Rather, the intent is to show popular culture is a vehicle through which social problems emerge, are defined, debated, and sometimes remedied. Whether or not you, the reader, specifically view *Tinder* or popular movies and music as causing social harm, there are other people out there who do and they actively seek to spread their message, oftentimes via popular culture, in an effort to get us to take notice of the problem they have discovered. Likewise, their opponents – in this example those who think *Tinder* does not produce social harm – will attempt to convince us that no social problem exists and we should have as much casual sex as possible. This process by which some people try to convince us that problems exist and others rebut those assertions is called the sociology of social problems, and it is our starting point.

The sociology of social problems

Throughout the book we will discuss how and why social problems come about and make their way into the public consciousness. We must start by recognizing that there are plenty of things that *could* be social problems at any given time. Whether or not they actually become social problems, however, is often unrelated to the relative harm they pose. To this point, the famous sociologist Herbert Blumer once wrote that "the pages of history are replete with instances of dire social conditions unnoticed and unattended in the societies in which they occurred" (1971: 302). By this he means social problems are not necessarily identified because they are objectively destructive to society, but rather because members of a population collectively define certain issues as social problems. Joel Best, a sociologist and leading scholar in the study of social problems, was among those who built on Blumer's idea that social problems are subjectively identified:

It is not an objective quality of a social condition, but rather the subjective reactions to that condition, that make something a social problem. Therefore, social problems should not be viewed as a type of social condition, but as a process of responding to social conditions. (Best, 2013: 9-10)

In other words, people come to diagnose, understand, and attach meaning to social problems like climate change, racism, and income inequality either directly through firsthand experience or indirectly from things like media reports, word-of-mouth, and reading books. To clarify this point, imagine you are sitting in a room full of people and the person next to you introduces himself as Dr. Hannibal Lecter. Upon recognizing the fictionalized cannibal murderer (*The Silence of the Lambs*, *Red Dragon*) had somehow come to life, many of you might politely excuse yourselves and get as far away from him as possible; yet some others might be sufficiently fascinated by the situation to strike up a conversation with Lecter. Regardless of your choice, the fact that another human being is seated next to you – in this case Hannibal Lecter – in a room full of people is an objective reality. But how you choose to interpret that scenario is purely subjective, based on whether you have identified the situation as problematic and fled to safety or been so charmed by Lecter's pleasant demeanor that you overlook his criminal tendencies (and perhaps end up being his dinner).

By applying the Lecter scenario to real-world situations, we can start to see how objective social conditions are subjectively defined as social problems. Consider the ongoing debate about global warming and whether man-made climate change is harmful to human existence. On one hand, it is a proven scientific fact that temperatures are progressively rising and the planet is getting warmer; so in that sense, global warming is an objective fact. Yet, although the vast majority of scientific experts and many citizens have concluded that these changing temperatures are a source of potential and already realized harm, skeptics suggest that fact alone is not sufficient to constitute a social problem. The fact that there is no absolute consensus that the objective social condition of climate change is actually a social problem means there is plenty of room for subjective debate about whether the problem is real, what it looks like, and what we should do about it. Whatever your own personal thoughts on the matter, the point is, we all make subjective determinations based on our perceptions of global warming and whether we think its perceived harms are real. And this brings us to an important question:

What influences our subjective judgments about whether objectively existing phenomenon are indeed social problems?

To a degree, our moral values and personal interests shape how we see the world. However, it is also important to consider the social and historical contexts in which social problems emerge in the public conscious, because something that is considered harmful at one point in time might be viewed much differently in another era. After all, the ancient Greek philosopher Socrates was essentially condemned to death for the crime of free thought, a virtue most westernized people now cherish. Specifically, Socrates was convicted of corrupting the minds of youth through spiritual teachings that failed to recognize and show proper deference to the gods recognized by the city of Athens, which supposedly inspired his students to rebuke the existing social order in defiance of the state. In his search for knowledge and wisdom, Socrates had questioned the status quo, and in ancient Greece this was considered a crime. This view still persists in some parts of the world, as evidenced by the case of Malala Yousafzai, a Pakistani activist who, in 2009, was hired by the British Broadcasting Corporation (BBC) at the age of 11 to write a diary about life under Taliban rule. Focusing mostly on a decree that the education of girls be banished as per Sharia law, Yousafzai would soon become a global champion for human rights and educational opportunities for women and children in Pakistan. By 2011, Yousafzai was nominated for the International Children's Peace Prize and was conferred a National Peace Award (since renamed the National Malala Peace Prize) by the Pakistani government. Beginning with her BBC-sponsored citizen journalism, the young teenager ultimately became recognized as a symbol of Taliban resistance and an important global voice for female equality. It also made her a target of Taliban militants. On October 9, 2012, assassins stopped Yousafzai's vehicle as she was returning home from school and proceeded to shoot her in the head and neck for the crime of promoting secularism in Pakistan. Fortunate to survive her injuries, Yousafzai would later win the 2014 Nobel Peace Prize, making her the youngest ever Nobel laureate.

Yousafzai's tale is important because it exemplifies how and why timing helps determine whether a particular condition is a viable social problem by facilitating the political and cultural opportunities needed for those issues to become culturally relevant. Yet there also needs to be people and groups like Socrates and Yousafzai, who take it upon themselves to make "assertions of grievances and claims" that communicate their concerns about prospective social problems to the public (Spector and Kitsuse, 1987: 75). When successful, these *claims-makers* draw attention to their issues by provoking mass media coverage, which provides much needed public recognition, rallying supporters into action, overcoming opponents who distribute competing claims, legitimizing the issue's standing as a social problem, and mobilizing public institutions into action to rectify the presumed harm (Blumer, 1971; Spector and Kitsuse, 1987; Best, 2008).

This interplay between competing claims-makers and the mass media sources needed to distribute their ideas means that claims must be framed in culturally resonant ways that influence both individual and collective action (Gitlin, 1980; Hilgartner and Bosk, 1988; Snow et al, 1986; Gamson et al, 1992; Binder, 1993; Benford and Hunt, 2003). For this reason, claims are more likely to be recognized as legitimate when they are infused within the popular culture of everyday life and "piggyback" on dramatic real-world events that direct public attention to the problem (see Ungar, 1992). The Westboro Baptist Church (WBC) offers a good example of how piggybacking works to draw attention to even the most incendiary problem claims. The WBC and its members have received scathing criticism in recent years for picketing the funerals of slain American military soldiers and murder victims in protest against society's growing acceptance of homosexuality. You may wonder why a group of people would do something so insensitive. The answer is simple: recognition and media coverage. While most people may frown upon the actions taken by the WBC, they have nonetheless been tremendously successful in becoming recognizable for branding a publicity stunt so extreme in nature that it has induced a social response.

Because social issues like global warming, racism, and homophobia do not simply exist in a vacuum waiting for people to discover them, they must be brought to the public's attention in ways that get as many people as possible to take notice. The broad reach and wide accessibility of popular culture makes it a potent tool for those interested in promoting a social problem because it influences what people consume, how they look, feel, act, and even their beliefs about what is right and wrong in the world. It can be helpful to think about social problems as being marketed to us in a manner similar to commercial products, like when competing car dealerships try to convince potential customers that they sell better performing automobiles at a more affordable price. Both have an objective commodity (the car) but must advertise themselves to the unique needs and concerns of the customer, while also convincingly demonstrating that shopping at another dealership will only lead to hardship and regret. In much the same way, problematic social conditions like racism or gendered inequality objectively exist. However, their simple existence is not sufficient for the larger society to consider them problematic and generate enough concern to merit a collective response. Think about an issue like human slavery. Even though it is almost universally loathed in westernized nations as an abuse of basic human rights, it nonetheless has existed for centuries and continues to persist in some parts of the world, including underground sex trafficking, which plagues even the most modernized areas of the United States and Europe.

The point is that we are surrounded every day by a lot of really bad stuff, and throughout our lives we are constantly diverting our attention away from that really bad stuff because we have jobs, families, friends, and a variety of other things to keep us busy or entertained. Politicians, activists, and other social actors, therefore, are a lot like those car dealers – their goal is to highlight something in society that they deem problematic and induce a widespread public response that forces policymakers to take action. According to Farhad Manjoo (2008), the seminal issue is the ease by which opinion in modern society can be certified as fact, thereby allowing most anyone to become a lay expert by simply going out and finding information that validates his or her beliefs, even if it contradicts established scientific truth. By consequence, our individual understanding of social problems and whether (and how) society as a whole chooses to combat them are not necessarily the product of objective truth, but rather by the *facts* we choose to believe often without even realizing we are merely parroting the information and claims imparted on us via news, social media, and, quite often, popular culture.

Linking social problems and popular culture

When Jon Stewart retired as host of *The Daily Show* in 2015, *The New York Times* described his legacy as having "changed journalism in the public arena for the responsibility of educating adult Americans on the truths of their day, regardless of ratings and sensationalism" (Lett, 2015). Such praise is both profound and curious given that Stewart is a comedian and not a journalist, and *The Daily Show* is an entertainment-based satirical "fake" news program. Yet it was not without merit – polling data indicate Americans that watch cable news tend to be less informed about current events than viewers of *The Daily Show* (see Rapoza, 2011). These days, the places most people traditionally turn to to get news about the pressing matters of the day, are starting to look and feel a lot more like entertaining talk shows, which favor sensationalism over substance and immediacy over depth. Although the most tangible effect of this modern media culture is a declining standard of news quality, there are practical reasons for the growing prevalence of pop culture infused *infotainment*. One result is that news programming has come to increasingly emphasize entertainment in hopes of maintaining audiences by providing brief, unambiguous narratives that contain plenty of visual action, dramatic conflict, and emotion (Snow 1983; Altheide, 1995; 2002). On any given day, you are likely to see a story about the latest Taylor Swift Twitter feud or Donald Trump's unique hairstyle alongside reports about real-world problems, and all of them can be cast as matters of pressing social concern. We may also see the intersections of popular culture and social problems on billboards and other signs we drive by during the daily commute to work or school. Clothing, bracelets and other items that people wear also convey their support or opposition to some social condition offer yet more examples of social problems being filtered through mechanisms of popular culture

Given that popular culture plays such a crucial role as a source of both information about and engagement with social issues in modern society, the core argument in this book is fairly straightforward – messages about social problems that get filtered through popular culture play a critically important role in how we identify and prioritize the social problems that concern us individually and as society as a whole. Once we recognize this fact it becomes easier to grapple with the idea that popular culture is much more than merely a casual reference to consumerism and the diversions of daily life; rather, it is an aspect of modern society that is loaded with core social processes and important messages about the world and our place in it. In the chapters that follow, we seek to do a few things: demonstrate the ubiquity and everyday influences of popular culture; provide an overview of core concepts and research findings derived from scholarship – particularly from the fields of sociology and media studies – devoted to the study of social problems and of popular culture; and use these core concepts and research findings as a foundation for a conceptual framework that identifies and explores important linkages between the products and processes of popular culture and the structured arrangements through which we identify, understand, and respond to social problems.

The analytical structure of the book is organized around four core intersections between popular culture and the social problems process:

(1) blaming; (2) spreading; (3) pushback; and (4) marketing. The first linkage of *blaming* popular culture for the existence of social problems is fairly straightforward, focusing attention on the various ways that public officials and activists argue that some aspect of popular culture is the cause of a particular social ill. If blaming is akin to scapegoating, the second aspect, *spreading*, can be understood as a form of propaganda designed to promote a particular point of view in efforts to sway or manipulate the public's understanding of social problems. The concept of spreading directs us to the ways that popular culture is often used as a mechanism of institutional power by political and bureaucratic actors to convey their preferred narratives about the causes of a social problem and what we should do about it. Third is *pushback*, which provides a means of examining how popular culture can serve as a vehicle for interpretations and claims that challenge dominant societal conceptions of social problems. The fourth and final linkage is *marketing* and deals with how social problems are advertised or sold to the public, and how such practices help to build and reinforce symbolic communities of support via popular culture. While simple in design, this framework will allow readers to better understand that popular culture helps define what social problems become recognized by the public, the subsequent discussions and debates over those issues, and the ultimate public and policy responses designed to rectify the perceived harm.

Throughout the chapters that follow, the book will explore a wide array of popular cultural forms and analyze the way that each intersects with social problems – guided by the core processes outlined in this chapter – in a way that articulates the specific ways in which pop culture influences how we identify, make sense of, and attempt to deal with troubling social issues. By navigating the complex role of popular culture in social life, the book will reveal the many ways that fads and fashions cultivate both individuality and conformity, while also addressing how pop culture can be used to manipulate public attention, attitudes, and beliefs. Finally, this text will hopefully challenge readers to think about how the critical examination of popular culture can reveal why the issues we perceive as social problems at any given time might be more the products of our cultural tastes than a reflection on the actual harms posed by the supposed threat.

TWO

Understanding Social Problems
and Popular Culture

If every reader of this book were to make a list of all the social problems existing in the world today, some of them would probably be fairly universal, like terrorism, violent crime, and racism. For other issues, objective consensus would be much more difficult to identify, as evidenced by the ongoing disputes about global warming and whether man-made climate change is indeed a social problem. No matter how many things you put on your list, there will always be someone who disagrees or other potential problems that you fail to recognize. Even more, if you were to compare your list with another person who lives down the street or even across the globe – or perhaps one that was written many years in the past – it would become clear that we do not all see social problems the same way. In other words, social problems are situational and subject to interpretation. Scary things like tainted Halloween candy, road rage, and random crime tend to be recognized as social problems in certain moments but not others. Even social problems that seem to exist in perpetuity, like racial discrimination and sexism, are often debated as if their existence cannot be factually documented. Moreover, some social problems are seen as "global" threats – such as terrorism or climate change, while others become defined as more localized concerns. This is precisely why mass shootings are generally characterized as a uniquely American problem, even though similar violent crimes can (and do) occur in other countries.

From these general observations a few important questions can be asked: Why do some prospective ills come to be universally defined as social problems? Why are other troubling conditions sometimes considered "someone else's problem" even when their objective existence can be found in virtually all corners of human existence? As importantly, how do each of us as individuals come to recognize social problems and their effect on our lives? And, of course, considering the focus of this book: What does popular culture have to do with all of this?

In order to answer these questions, we must recognize that everything we come into contact with in the social world influences our individual perceptions of reality. Knowledge can be acquired through direct experience, such as going to a museum or base-jumping off a cliff; or it can be symbolically obtained through shared knowledge in a variety of ways, including family and peer socialization, formal schooling, and mass media, which explains how we can know about things like walking on the moon or anything else we have never personally confronted. From the moment we are born, the process of social learning begins, and as we grow older our interactions with the world routinely influence what we think about others and ourselves, including all the things we believe are good and bad. For this reason, it is useful to think in terms of *objective reality*, or what is actually happening in the world at any given moment, and our *subjective perceptions of reality*, which is how people process, make sense of, and give meaning to what is actually happening in the world.

This idea that we subjectively attach meaning to social phenomena that exist objectively, is both important and at times confusing, because often it is easy to conclude that the world simply exists as we see it through the unique lens of our individual lives. For most of us it is likely unfathomable that the Nazi regime could have coerced so many Germans into supporting the atrocities of the Holocaust. Likewise, it might be difficult to understand the mindset of a radical ISIS jihadist, or how and why someone can fly planes into buildings and murder innocent people. Yet the truth is that nobody was ever born a Nazi or a jihadist; they were socialized toward a particular worldview that skewed their perceptions of reality towards something that most people believe to be perverse. For this reason, an ISIS member would likely define a jihadist movement as righteous, while most everyone else would view those actions as terrorism. Although they would be describing the same objective act (a jihadist movement), the social meaning being attached is quite different (righteous vs. terrorism). Through this example we see that our personal sense of reality takes shape based on the information we receive and the ways we interpret that knowledge; and for this reason, the ways in which we make sense of social issues are influenced by our own personal experiences, as well as the structural conditions of society and the swirl of cultural forces we encounter throughout our lives.

Box 2.1 Benghazi, news media, and public opinion

The 2012 attack on American diplomats in Benghazi, Libya, which left 10 people injured and four dead, including US Ambassador J. Christopher Stevens, was not initially characterized in the press as a planned terrorist ambush, even though many conservative politicians and pundits were espousing that position from the beginning (The Center for Media and Public Affairs, 2012). Persistent coverage by Fox News framing the strike as an act of terror (Baier, 2012), and a string of Congressional investigative hearings would eventually shift the media narrative toward one that questioned why the State Department did not take proper security precautions, despite knowing that diplomatic personnel in the Benghazi region were being threatened by extremists prior to the attack.

One of the prominent Benghazi narratives advanced in Fox News coverage was that the attack had been trivialized thanks to "liberal media spin" bent on protecting President Obama and his administration for failing to take adequate preventative action.

> In the real world, when you cover up four murders after the fact, you likely go to [prison]. In government, you retire with dignity and run for president with full media support...The Obama administration has lied, stonewalled, bullied, and intimidated – the true marks of an open and transparent administration. And with few notable exceptions, the American media haven't just let them get away [with] it. Heck, they've helped... It wasn't just the traditional media spinning for Team Obama. Lefty outlets did their darndest to downplay the death of four Americans, including the only US ambassador killed since 1979. (Gainor, 2013)

By all accounts, Fox News audiences overwhelmingly accepted this version of events. Among those who regularly watch or get news online from Fox News, 55% believe that Obama has acted dishonestly, and among Republican audiences, that figure rises to a whopping 79%. By contrast, only 28% of those who do not regularly watch Fox News feel that Obama has been deceitful about the Benghazi incident; and among Republicans that do not regularly watch Fox News, the percentage of respondents who believe Obama has acted dishonestly lowers to 60% (Pew Research Center, 2013). These partisan audience responses to Benghazi mirror other social issues because where an audience chooses to get their news – and consume claims – strongly influences how they interpret current events, social problems, political matters, and all other aspects of social life.

Thinking about social problems: key concepts and themes

In many ways, how we interpret and respond to prospective social problems is inescapably linked to the fundamental desire most people have to conform to accepted cultural mores and social standards. Still, people sometimes do and say things that come into conflict with widely accepted values. This can occur in a variety of ways, such as violating the law through criminal behavior, acting in a distasteful but not illegal manner, or even innocently deviating from commonly shared social norms, like when someone invades your personal space or wears age-inappropriate clothing. At times, people deliberately engage in these sorts of disruptive behaviors as a way of getting attention or communicating a message. This was evident when Occupy Wall Street activists held large public rallies to protest economic inequality. The reason these protesters chose to publicly (and purposefully) disturb shared norms was because their efforts helped attract recognition to their chosen social problem and bring it to the attention of the larger population. And this is important because social problems are not necessarily identified because of the objective harm they impose on society, but rather because members of a society come to collectively define certain issues as social problems (Blumer, 1971). That is, people come to recognize, understand, and attach meaning to social problems either directly through firsthand experience or indirectly from things like media reports, word of mouth, and the activities of activists.

Think for a moment about how most people obtain information about horrific crimes like mass and school shootings. Whether it is Columbine, Virginia Tech, or someone "going postal," by now you probably know the storyline all too well. One of the more vivid examples in recent years occurred when James Holmes walked into an Aurora, Colorado, movie theater in July of 2012 and opened fire, killing 12 people and injuring 58 others. A few months later the horrific Sandy Hook elementary school shooting took place, in which Adam Lanza gunned down his mother, six school staff, and 20 young children in Newtown, Connecticut. All told, there were 62 mass shootings in the United States that involved four or more fatalities between 1982 and 2012 (Follman et al, 2012).

Much in line with public perceptions, some research shows these incidents are occurring more frequently in recent years (Cohen et al, 2014); yet other scholars suggest the rate of mass shootings in the United States has remained remarkably stable (about 20 per year) since 1976 (Fox, 2013).

Given this lack of consensus and the terrifying menace of an insane gunman mowing down innocent victims for what often seems like random reasons, it is perhaps unsurprising that gun control has become a "hot button" issue in American politics. Legislators, lobbyists, and concerned citizens continue to debate the reasons why mass shootings occur and the ways to keep citizens safe. Pressure groups like the National Rifle Association (NRA) and the Coalition to Stop Gun Violence bombarding audiences with competing messages about guns being either the cause of crime or the cure to increasing public safety. Even people who do not watch the news or follow current events are likely to confront the issue when watching their favorite primetime television shows and feature films with "ripped from the headlines" storylines that offer plenty of gun violence.

Yet for all the public concern and debate about gun control, Neil Steinberg of the *Chicago Sun-Times* notes the amount of cultural attention dedicated to mass shootings is disproportionately high.

> What mass shootings are is dramatic – deranged gunman bursting into public places murdering innocents for no reason at all. That catches and holds the public's attention, certainly more than random individuals falling off ladders or slipping in bathtubs do, and the truth of the situation – 38 percent of the people who die in the United States die from accidents, versus .003 percent who die in mass shootings – does nothing to change the attention the media lavishes on the subject. (Steinberg, 2013)

Data further suggest that while mass shootings do occur in the United States with alarming frequency compared to other westernized nations, the chances of being victimized are remarkably low. Between 2006 and 2012, for example, the FBI identified 184 mass shooting victims, while during those years the total US population surpassed 300,000,000 (Kepple et al, 2013). Furthermore, the odds of actually dying in a school shooting are estimated at greater than one in 1,000,000 (Bloom, 2012). What we have, then, are objective events – the actual shootings – being fused with subjective interpretations that are fueled by cultural messages disseminated through news reports, public officials, gun advocates, victims' families, and so forth, many of which cultivate public fear by exaggerating the problem so much that many people come to believe that victimization in a mass shooting is inevitable.

Undoubtedly these sorts of crimes are tragic and lead to regrettable loss of life – particularly when children are involved – yet the question remains as to why mass and school shootings are widely considered severe social problems, when they occur with such relative infrequency and directly affect so few people, while other illegal behaviors like white collar crime yield more diffusive and widespread harm but are often overlooked. The answer is simple – acts of violence intersect with the sorts of fear-laden cultural narratives that resonate with the average citizen. For instance, a case of embezzlement or corrupt Wall Street bankers might elicit genuine outrage, but it pales in comparison to the way violent crime captures the public's attention and imagination, which helps explain why coverage of murders are far more prominent in news and entertainment than stories about money laundering. You can be sure that public officials, activists, and even entertainers are well aware of this fact, so in those moments when people are feeling most vulnerable or scared, they are likely to be bombarded with claims about the causes of such horrible violence and what we must do to recalibrate the moral order in our society.

From a sociological perspective, the study of social problems therefore begins with people and groups making claims about the harms caused by an objective real-world phenomenon in hopes of convincing the larger public to take notice and collectively identify it as a social problem. When successful, mass media coverage then provides much needed public recognition, helping to rally advocates into action, legitimizing the issue's standing as a social problem, and mobilizing public institutions into action to rectify the presumed social harm. For this reason, claimants and activists must always be "alert and ready to take advantage of ...

opportune moments" to advance their agendas (Best, 2008: 79). This is precisely why, for example, proponents and opponents of fossil fuel production will have an easier time finding an audience for their claims following a mining disaster, oil rig explosion, or rapid rise in gas prices.

Given this reality, the goal of any public figure trying to convince us that a social problem merits our attention is to produce a message that is sufficiently newsworthy to journalists, while eliciting concern, fear, and outrage from the general public. One of the more common ways that this is accomplished is by emphasizing shared values and moral principles, which draw on common beliefs that tend to evoke a strong, visceral reaction. Often these attempts to manipulate our emotions can be difficult to recognize because even though the claims themselves might be completely outlandish they are routinely used in news reports without even a hint of cynicism. This helps to give credibility to a whole host of manufactured fears, ranging from Sarah Palin's idea that the Affordable Care Act (Obamacare) would create bureaucratic "death panels" that determine whether elderly Americans merit continued medical care, to mall escalators that unexpectedly stop, and exotic pets who pose a disease threat "that could rival a terrorist attack" (Associated Press, 2006).

Box 2.2: Boko Haram and the #BringBackOurGirls movement

When the Islamic terrorist collective Boko Haram kidnapped 276 schoolgirls from the Chibok region of Nigeria in April of 2014, it set off a global firestorm of anger and protest, most notably characterized by the #BringBackOurGirls online movement. Initiated shortly after the kidnappings when a lawyer named Ibrahim Abdullah posted #BringBackOurGirls in a tweet, the hashtag soon went viral and "would go on to become one of Africa's most popular online campaigns, which was shared more than four million times over the next month on Twitter" (AFP, 2016). The campaign was endorsed by hundreds of celebrities and influential public figures, including Michelle Obama, Ellen DeGeneres, Salma Hayek, Antonio Banderas, Harrison Ford, Sean "Puff Daddy" Combs, Alicia Keys, and countless others, many of whom published photos of themselves holding signs and placards with the bring back our girls hashtag (or, alternatively, the slogan "Real Men Don't Buy Girls").

Aside from about 60 of girls who managed to escape, the whereabouts of the remaining Chibok victims remains unknown; and their abduction is not an isolated act. "It is estimated that at least 2,000 women and girls have been kidnapped since the start of 2014. Boys and young men have also been taken" (Nagarajan, 2015). All told, the fight against Boko Haram in Nigeria "since 2009 has claimed at least 20,000 lives and made more than 2.6 million others homeless" (AFP, 2016). Several years after #BringBackOurGirls went viral it is unlikely you will still see celebrities advocating for the Chibok victims, their families, or the people of Nigeria. There are still websites and activist groups advocating for actions to be taken against Boko Haram, and stronger measures adopted to locate the missing, and Nigerian President Goodluck Jonathon lost reelection in 2015 largely due to perceived governmental inaction following the Chibok abductions (Nagarajan, 2015). However, #BringBackOurGirls is mostly gone from the public conscious as media attention has shifted to more newsworthy current events and social problems.

For all its hype, we may ask whether hashtag campaigns like #BringBackOurGirls are meaningfully helping to combat terrorist groups like Boko Haram and other pressing social problems. There is no denying that the internet offers claimants the unique ability to pique a rapid mobilized response when communicating claims about issues that resonate with audiences, which are adopted by celebrities and other public figures, and attract media interest. Yet as the #BringBackOurGirls campaign reveals, the dynamism of online technology does not alter the underlying reality of the social problems process. Claims become irrelevant if people stop listening to them and their messenger – even if those social problems continue unabated. The internet, then, provides new ways to spread the word, but does not make those claims inherently worthy of public sympathy if the claims-makers themselves are unable to remain socially relevant (see Maratea, 2014).

According to sociologist Barry Glassner, these sorts of hyperbolic claims are not outliers, but rather reflect how people are "bamboozled about serious concerns" (1999: 3) by public officials, activists, and social institutions like news and entertainment media, each of whom profit to some degree by selling us fear. In fact, Glassner argues, "we have so many fears, many of them off-base" because we are constantly inundated "with sensationalistic stories designed to increase ratings" and make money (1999: xx). Of course, while the media's constant need for novel material makes them receptive to stories about a whole host of things we should fear, ranging from legitimate issues like climate change, to the seemingly absurd, there are more people and groups in any moment trying to get our attention than there is time to report on all of their claims. Accordingly, the cultural spotlight only shines on the select few issues that find residence in the daily news cycles and popular entertainment media.

Thinking about popular culture: key concepts and themes

Popularized fears, then, begin to take shape when claims about the existence of certain social problems are circulated through society, often through mass media, and attain sufficient cultural relevance for people to take notice of them. In many ways, we are consumers of the social problems funneled to us in everyday life through popular or mass culture. According to John Fiske, popular culture is "more a culture of process than of products" that "serves the interest of 'the people'" within a given society (1995: 323). By this he means that popular culture furnishes the material and cultural commodities that appeal to the mass population, such as music, movies, fashion, and so forth; but it also facilitates the "social circulation of meanings, values, and pleasures" that underpin "the processes of forming social identities and social relationships" (Fiske, 1995: 322). Through popular culture, people are able to socially locate relevant fads and trends and adopt (or reject) them as a means of expressing their individual and shared identity within society. This can include personal fashion styles, technological preferences, preferred forms of entertainment, and is even reflected in everyday interactions, like the way people greet each other and the slang they use among friends. In this way, popular culture functions as a benchmark by which people cultivate the self-image they project to others.

But most of all, the popular culture of everyday life is driven by consumerism and mass media. Although popular culture reflects the interests of average citizens, it simultaneously serves the economic benefit of the dominant class by coercing passive acceptance of standardized cultural commodities and goods that legitimate certain values, norms, interests, and pleasures while rejecting others (see Fiske, 1995). As far back as 1964, the German philosopher Herbert Marcuse noted that culture continuously informs (and controls) our thoughts, beliefs, values, and needs because it is designed to facilitate the mass consumption of false needs. To Marcuse, false needs are the unsophisticated material goods we acquire to satisfy desires marketed to us as vital to our happiness – like wanting a new Playstation or the biggest possible television – while diverting our attention from the things we really need in life, such as the freedom and autonomy to live our lives liberated from the very social control forces spread through society via culture. Marcuse's colleagues, Theodor Adorno and Max Horkheimer, were also critical of popular culture, comparing what they described as the *culture industry* to the factory production of standardized goods with "commercially produced meanings embedded in expressive works that include text, audio, and video," and which provoke docile acceptance among the larger population that consume them (Kidd, 2014: 7, see also Horkheimer and Adorno, [1944] 2002). They argue that popular culture distracts people, through entertainment, from the reality that society engulfs us in a world of fear, instability, war, and other potentially destabilizing social problems: "Mass-consciousness can be molded" by those in power "only because the masses 'want this stuff'" (see Adorno, 2006: 81, see also Adorno, 1941). The result is an insidious and covert form of social control, which is tied to a culture industry that offers people little more than the "freedom to be the same" (Horkheimer and Adorno, [1944] 2002: 136). That is, culture spawns a passive audience of conformist consumers who are repeatedly told each and every day about what they need to make their lives better and the how they should respond to the social and political matters that are most pertinent to their lives (see Adorno, 2001; Horkheimer and Adorno, [1944] 2002).

Adorno, Horkheimer, and Marcuse basically conceptualized how and why people perceive cultural and technological advancements as liberating them to live better and more comfortable lives, when they actually expose citizens to greater bureaucratic and corporate control. Nowhere is this fact more evident than in cyberspace, where we have freedom to buy all sorts of things, from the most mundane of household goods to the kinkiest sex toys, all from the privacy of home. We can participate with relative anonymity in a free flowing exchange of ideas, and can even develop false cyber-personas altogether. Yet online technology also makes us more visible than ever before to government surveillance, corporate marketing, pedophiles' hopes to seduce young children, identity thieves, and scam artists that lurk in the shadows of the information superhighway. Modern popular culture also markets for our consumption incidents of *self-surveillance*, whereby private citizens monitor and sometimes exploit the actions of other people. Go online and you can probably find videos of famous people like Kim Kardashian and former Vice-Presidential candidate John Edwards engaging in pornographic acts; these celebrity "sex tapes" are often unauthorized and reflect the extent to which modern technology can expose our most intimate affairs. We have also seen the prevalence of dashboard cameras and cellphone videos documenting incidents of police and citizen misconduct; and shows like *Tosh.O* draw their humor from mocking people exposed publicly for doing stupid things in online viral videos. The point is that popular culture clarifies for a society the acceptable modes of appearance, behavior, and conduct; and as technology advances, we all run a greater risk of being exposed, mocked, stigmatized, shamed, or punished for violating mainstream social norms.

Our intent here is not to compare a humorous cellphone video of someone being foolish with a sinister dashcam recording of a police officer shooting an unarmed African American. Rather, it is important to conceptualize popular culture (and the culture industry) as a focal lens for what is socially valued by dominant society at any given time, which exerts considerable pressure on average citizens to not only passively conform, but to also keep wanting more and more of the cultural commodities produced for their consumption. So in a manner of speaking, it is culture that creates and reinforces *meaning* in everyday life, which shapes everything from our political ideologies and moral foundations to personal style and leisurely interests (see Kidd, 2014). Yet, because so much of what we experience via popular culture is at the forefront of public life in one moment and relegated to the dustbin of history in the next, it can be difficult to keep up with all of the ways that mass culture truly affects our lives. Sure, fads and fashions tend to come and go — today nobody is concerned like parents were in the 1950s that Elvis Presley's swiveling hips would send young women into uncontrolled sexual frenzy; and there are no kids begging their parents to get them the latest Cabbage Patch Kid doll or Atari video game like during the 1980s. These trends have been replaced by demand for the latest iPhone and iPad, the musical popularity of Taylor Swift and "boy bands," and fears that movies like *Straight Outta Compton* will lead to increases in social violence.

In truth, though, the more things change as society continues to progress, popular culture nonetheless remains remarkably stable and profoundly influential, even if much of what we experience in popular culture might sometimes seem "trivial, ephemeral, tacky, and lacking in scholarly and academic merit" (Grazian, 2010: ix). To be fair, it is understandable if people deride the caricaturized visions of real life presented in shows like *Here Comes Honey Boo Boo*, *Keeping up with the Kardashians*, and *Jersey Shore*; and it is easy to think that we alone are responsible for our personal style, entertainment preferences, and more generally, how we present ourselves to others. But in doing so we run the risk of overlooking the fact that mass culture possesses considerable power in the public sphere: "It can generate political commentary and activism, mirror changing social values and societal practices, resist mainstream hegemonies, and ... it both shapes and reflects our ideals" (Fedorak, 2009: 4-5). Fiske (2010) adds that popular culture reflects how individuals and groups attempt to maintain their own distinct social and cultural identities in an increasingly homogenous, globalized world. One need look no further for evidence of this fact than the popularity of rap, hip-hop, and urban fashion trends that act simultaneously as entertainment and expressions of cultural unity on issues like drugs, gangs, race relations, social inequality, and political empowerment.

Through popular culture, the power to resist authority and the institutional establishment is strengthened by the acknowledgement of shared identity, which is not only essential in the fight to combat social problems, but is also necessary to change widespread public beliefs and coerce bureaucratic change. It can be quite difficult to effect social change on our own as individuals. But through popular culture, various ideas, voices, and actions can unite, forming a more powerful sort of collective response to shared concerns. To put this idea into context, imagine for a moment that you are an activist standing on a street corner warning passersby about all of the dangers of bad dental hygiene. It is doubtful that your efforts would lead to a world of cleaner teeth because your audience would be limited to all of the people physically in your presence, and perchance anyone who records you using a smart phone and shares the video. Now perhaps a local news affiliate picks up on your efforts and interviews you for a segment on the nightly news, and that story subsequently airs during network news broadcasts, compelling cable news outlets to seek you out for their own reports on the need to brush regularly and have minty fresh breath. Suddenly, the audience exposed to your message has expanded exponentially and you have attained an element of credibility as an expert on dental health. Your story has now become so recognizable that it becomes a feature film with you as the central character fighting evil candy company executives who have hatched a secret plan to control the world by destroying everyone's teeth. Soon you have become such an inspiration that Bono writes a melodramatic song in your honor and people show their support for your cause by purchasing and wearing your collection of "Toothstrong" shirts and wrist bracelets. While this is an admittedly exaggerated illustration, the point is that popular culture can – and often does – play a crucial role in transforming individual ideas and actions into widely recognized social concerns.

In this sense, collective unity, as expressed through popular culture, can be a source of empowerment, particularly for traditionally marginalized people and groups. All of this becomes particularly relevant when we consider the extent to which we judge others and ourselves according to the fads, fashions, and technologies that are culturally valued at any given time. It is not that any person cannot survive without an iPad, fancy car, designer clothing, or a really large house. Rather, we desire them because they reflect cultural markers or success and prestige. In many ways, the essence of popular culture is found in our collective efforts to become one with the most immediate and contemporary aspects of everyday life, whether that be by sporting shoes with a Nike "swoosh," holding a handbag that displays the iconic "DG" of Dolce & Gabbana, downloading the latest and greatest music and video games, or even taking sides when debating the most pressing social and political problems. That is, until the next most important thing comes along and makes your shoes, handbag, or social problem obsolete.

You can observe a lot just by watching

"Life moves pretty fast," notes Ferris Bueller in the film *Ferris Bueller's Day Off*, "If you don't stop to look around once in a while you could miss it." His own movie exploits included skipping school to drive a fast sports car, attending a baseball game, dining at a fine restaurant, taking in a parade, and enjoying a relaxing dip in the pool – all leisurely aspects of popular culture, which similarly offers the rest of us "intrinsic and extrinsic rewards and the opportunity to escape from the stresses of everyday life" (Fedorak, 2009: 4). Most of you are probably well versed in the ways that popular culture provides a source of pleasure, which includes reading, even if you prefer to be doing something else right now. Yet sociologist David Rowe argues that there is a contradictory nature to popular culture, in that it is the source of all the swanky products marketed for our consumption, which reflect our collective conformity and distract us from the mundane or harsh realities of our daily existence, while also conveying messages about individualism, independence, and resistance to the status quo (Rowe, 1995).

Whether you are watching your favorite television show, listening to a song, or viewing athletes wear pink in solidarity against breast cancer, popular culture routinely directs public attention towards social problems and other real-world concerns. Back in the 1960s, for instance, it was trendy in literature and music to flaunt anti-authority and anti-war messages. Novels like Ken Kesey's *One Flew Over the Cuckoo's Nest* and protest-inspired tunes like Sam Cooke's *A Change is Gonna Come* were driven by the collective turmoil of the 1960s, and inspired young people to fight for social progress. Two decades later, Bruce Springsteen spoke to a whole new generation about the horrors of the Vietnam War and ill treatment of military veterans in his song *Born in the U.S.A.*; and by the 1990s, the explosion of urban culture allowed artists like Public Enemy and films like *Boyz n the Hood* to take aim at the continued existence of racial inequality and segregation in American society. Popular culture has also helped shine a spotlight on gendered inequality through films such as *Thelma & Louise*, which present strong female characters and challenge chauvinistic stereotypes about women. More recently, yellow "Livestrong" bracelets have raised awareness and money for cancer research, while programs like HBO's *Looking* and the Caitlyn Jenner inspired reality show *I am Cait*, reflect changing public attitudes about sexual orientation in the United States. Whether or not we stop to think about it, pop culture is perpetually shining a light on what is happening in contemporary society, allowing it to simultaneously mirror prevailing values and be a catalyst for social change. In doing so, popular culture does so much more than simply entertain; it is an all-encompassing force that unifies and divides, builds consensus and sparks disagreement, stimulates collective action, and crystallizes social reality, thereby prompting each of us as unique individuals to better understand our place in the world.

Popular culture also has intrinsic economic and symbolic value to its producers and those who have the power to strategically manipulate it to their benefit. Consider the National Football League (NFL) and its affiliate franchises, which produce billions of dollars in annual revenue by supplying a product that fans of American football cannot live without. Armed with tremendous cultural authority, thanks in part to its widespread popularity in the United States, the NFL's reach extends beyond the perceived entertainment value it provides fans. From a sociological perspective, for example, the NFL reflects deeply rooted patriarchal gendered stereotypes, with rugged male athletes displaying the value of heightened masculinity, and often being described by commentators as strong, brave, and fearless "leaders or men," while female cheerleaders waving pom-poms applaud from the sidelines in skimpy outfits. Although the NFL undoubtedly produces social good along with the seemingly never-ending parade of news reports about players being arrested for rape, domestic abuse, and other unsavory acts, the point is that the drivers of popular culture are much more than the commodities they produce and the enjoyment they provide.

The force will be with you, always

This brings us to the larger intellectual thread that runs through the remaining chapters of this book: when you remove the entertaining veneer of popular culture there is revealed a source of social power so formidable that it shapes a society's collective identity, promotes conformity, reasserts bureaucratic and corporate control, while also generating resistance to authority and provoking social change (Combs, 1984). Whether or not we recognize it amidst the hustle and bustle of everyday life, all of us are conduits to the power of popular culture; it flows to us from all of our face-to-face and mediated interactions with the social world, and through us to others with whom we come into contact. On one hand, there are elements of our relationship to popular culture that should be disconcerting to critical observers. The extent to which popular culture is intertwined with virtually all aspects of our public and private lives leaves us susceptible to manipulation by powerful actors, institutions, and corporations, who can spread their interests via popular culture and get us to buy their products or support social positions that benefit them – even if we are harmed in the process. But there is a bright side. The famed French philosopher Michel Foucault notes that while power is a ubiquitous, coercive force that spawns self-enforced discipline and conformity, it does not necessarily prohibit resistance, which he conceptualized as actions or behaviors in opposition to (or that question) the accepted, prevailing, or dominant social order

In truth, most readers of this book (and its authors) likely provide tacit support for some really bad things – like worker exploitation and docile conformity – by simple fact that you probably have or want a big television, nice cars, jewelry, and the trendiest fashion. Yet at the same time, many of you will also harness the power of popular culture as a vehicle for protest, resistance, and to, in the words of Public Enemy, "make everybody see in order to fight the powers that be." This is, in many ways, the fundamental contradiction of popular culture – it molds and reflects shared values that unify members of society while also inspiring individualism and non-conformity. Often the goods and styles recognized as trendy or chic emerged from the cultural fringes to become fashionable. While this might seem confusing, it really is quite simple and can really be visualized when your style, interests, speech, and so forth, evolve as fads and fashions change over time. Tattoos, for example, are an artistic form of individual expression, but have become so widespread and popular in recent decades that they have long since ceased to be unique. Shifts in popular culture have effectively rendered tattoos rather mainstream, even though people with excessive tattooing, such as people who are covered from head to toe, still exist outside of conventional standards and assert a unique expression of individuality. The point is that popular culture inescapably reflects both our shared conventionality with others and the qualities that make us individually distinct, and this includes how, when, and why we respond to social problems. And since there is no way to elude its powerful influence over your life, there is added value in critically understanding how popular culture shapes social reality, including all of the supposed evils that are presumably sending the world to hell in a handbasket. Because whether the social problem involves racism, sexism, economic inequality, or perhaps even the need to construct a real-life Death Star (for which an actual White House online petition garnered more than 34,000 signatures), you can be sure its existence in the public consciousness is never too far removed from popular culture.

Box 2.3: Communication technology and recycled fears

Mass media and communication technology are essential conduits of popular culture. Historically, advancements in both have been glorified for their role in advancing human society and simultaneously been viewed as socially harmful. In fact, the widespread praise *and* fear of mass media and technology is hardly a novel phenomenon; these concerns tend to reproduce themselves across generations. To put this idea into context, consider how public perceptions of early radio eerily mirrored both the hope and anxieties of the internet as a revolutionary force in contemporary society. The explosive growth of radio in the early to mid-20th century – from 400,000 sets owned in 1922 (.016 sets per household) to 176,000,000 sets by 1962 (3.22 per household) (see De Fleur, 1966: 66) – was viewed as innovative and transformative because unlike newspapers and other print media, radio offered audiences the *immediacy* to experience events in real time. And because corporate, governmental, and religious interests had no direct control over what audiences chose to listen to in their homes, the household radio was hailed as an inherently democratizing technology.

This ability to experience events as they happened made radio both transformative *and* led panicked skeptics to claim that radio would destroy the moral fabric of society. If people could listen to anything they wanted, they might become detached from their moral and spiritual link to the community. If that alone was not enough for some to fear the consequences of radio, they could be further swayed by the idea of vulnerable children being exposed to dangerous, amoral programming. Of course, nobody could really listen to *anything* they wanted. By 1923 there were over 500 major stations in operation across the country and approximately 1,400 small amateur ones that broadcast intermittently (De Fleur, 1966: 62), yet audiences were limited to hearing what operators of those stations chose to broadcast. Oftentimes, listeners could not hear anything at all because the sheer number of stations fighting for space on the dial meant that there were often several sharing the same

27

frequency, the result being that they cancelled out each other's signals. In order to resolve the glut, the federal government ultimately passed the Radio Act of 1927, which led to the corporatization of radio broadcasting. Amateurs who previously had the freedom to broadcast at their choosing on deregulated airwaves were soon overrun by burgeoning regional and coast-to-coast networks operated by big companies like the National Broadcasting Company (NBC) and the Columbia Broadcasting System (CBS) (Emery et al, 1973; Davis, 1974).

By the early 1940s, the voice of radio was, for better or worse, limited to a select group of elite broadcast corporations. This marked a major shift from its inception, when radio was not unlike the internet: a deregulated communication medium that allowed both corporate networks and "citizen broadcasters" alike equal access to the airwaves, and concurrently gave its audience the freedom to listen to any available programming at its choosing. In many ways the debate over *net neutrality* and possible consequences of corporate control of the information superhighway mirrors similar issues that were raised after the passage of the Radio Act of 1927; and fears that technologies like television and the internet are harming society tend to reproduce themselves from generation to generation with each subsequent technological advancement.

KEY QUESTIONS

Why do some social concerns become fully developed social problems while other concerns do not?

What is social problems claims-making? What role do mass media play in the creation and distribution of social problems claims?

How do our interactions with popular culture influence our perceptions of social problems?

What is the "culture industry"? How does it shape how popular culture forms are created and how likely we are to find those forms and engage with them?

SUGGESTED READINGS

Adorno, T.W. (2001) *The culture industry: Selected essays on mass culture* (2nd edn), New York, NY: Routledge.

Best, J. (2013) *Social problems* (2nd edn), New York: W.W. Norton and Company.

Childs, J.D. (2014) "'Let's talk about race': Exploring racial stereotypes using popular culture in social studies classrooms", *The Social Studies*, 105(6): 291-300.

THREE

Blaming Popular Culture for the Existence of Social Problems

One Friday evening in May of 2014, 22-year old Elliot Rodger embarked on a shooting spree in the beachside community of Isla Vista, California. His crimes quickly became a national news story, owing not only to the level of violence (six people were killed and 14 others were injured) but also to the novelty of the setting and the biography of the shooter. The community where it occurred, Isla Vista, is known for its unique mix of beach culture and college students – certainly not the sort of place where most people envision episodes of violent crime. Likewise, Rodger did not necessarily fit the typical profile associated with such wanton acts of violence. Although most mass shooters are white males, Rodger nonetheless embodied what many people believe to be "all-American" values – he was affluent, well educated, from a wealthy family, and had no known history of violence. Yet, investigators soon learned that this was a self-proclaimed "retribution" killing. Rodger was apparently distraught by the fact that he was still a virgin and sought revenge on females in his age group, noting in one video recorded before the attacks: "I will slaughter every single blonde slut I see!"

A media frenzy quickly followed as the press redirected its attention to yet another mass shooting in the United States. The term *media frenzy* refers to the swift and overwhelming rush of *breaking* news coverage that ensues when competing news agencies direct considerable resources and public attention toward a focal event, such as a mass shooting or terrorist attack (see Fox et al, 2007). Media frenzies by definition call for immediate and extensive reporting of issues and events even though there is usually very little accurate information available to sustain that coverage. This is important to consider when thinking about social problems because this style of news tends to spawn distorted and deeply flawed ideas about the issues being covered (Sacco, 2005; Monahan, 2010).

This is precisely how it played out in the coverage of the Isla Vista shooting. The 24-hour cable news networks quickly worked the story into their television programming while also providing updates through social media and online news sites. Broadcast networks and their affiliates jumped into the fray with updates during nightly newscasts, and discussed the matter at length on morning shows like *Today* and *Good Morning America*. Rodger's name was also splashed across newspaper and magazine headlines, while talk radio hosts debated the matter with their listeners. In cyberspace the shootings were also *trending*, with countless people discussing the incident and offering their own ideas about its causes and how to best protect society from this type of violent gun crime.

The sense of immediacy inherent to this sort of live and late-breaking coverage meant that lots of people were looking at these events and trying to make sense of them in real time. With the benefit of hindsight, we can see that virtually all of the media coverage following the Isla Vista shootings offered little insight into the actual causes of mass shootings. The responses from media figures, pundits, and political leaders largely focused on knee-jerk emotional reactions and morality-laden statements about guns, mental illness, video games, and a whole host of other possible explanatory factors, which are presented to audiences as the factual causes of mass shootings and violent crimes, despite a lack of actual evidence to support those assertions. All of this is important because media frenzies and the (mis)information they tend to produce indicate a typical trajectory through which popular culture becomes a focal point for those looking to make sense of troublesome social issues.

Box 3.1: Moral panics and popular culture

Media frenzies often precipitate (and cause) periods of heightened public fear that sociologists describe as moral panics, which refers to "collective feelings of outrage directed at a person, group, or event believed to represent a threat to the prevailing cultural values of a society" (Kavanaugh and Maratea, 2014: 378). Originally theorized by Stanley Cohen during the 1970s, moral panics focus on the role played by news media in generating fear and influencing public perceptions about social problems, as well as fostering moral indignation toward those problems (see Cohen, 2002). Cohen also stressed that while the social problems that gain notoriety during moral panics may not represent genuinely objective threats to society, the societal reactions to those are just as, if not more, important to understanding social problems like crime and deviance, than the threat itself (see Kavanaugh and Maratea, 2014).

Quite often, popular culture becomes a focal point for public reactions during the lifespan of moral panics. During the early 1980s, for example, fears spread rapidly that the role-playing board game Dungeons & Dragons was prompting adolescents to be "seduced into witchcraft," Satanism, anti-government insurgency, and commit violent rapes and murders (Michaud, 2015; Haberman, 2016). Although there was no actual evidence that the game was responsible for harming the lives of young people, an eruption of news coverage underpinned by real life events like the 1979 disappearance of a college student, and claims-makers who successfully attracted media attention to their concerns.

> In 1979, the game was linked to the disappearance of a college student named James Dallas Egbert III. ("Fantasy cult angle probed in search for computer whiz," read one headline.) Though he was eventually found unharmed, the episode was turned into "Mazes and Monsters," a potboiler by Rona Jaffe that was adapted into a 1982 TV movie starring Tom Hanks. Patricia Pulling, whose D & D-obsessed son committed suicide, started an organization called Bothered About Dungeons & Dragons (BADD). She later wrote a book called *The devil's web: Who is stalking your children for Satan?* Dr Thomas Radecki, a founding member of the National Coalition on TV Violence, said, "There is no doubt in my mind that the game Dungeons & Dragons is causing young men to kill themselves and others." In her book *Raising PG kids in an X-rated society*, Tipper Gore connected the game to satanism and the occult. All of this prompted a *60 minutes* segment in which [Gary Gygax, the game's co-founder]

rejected these myriad accusations, calling them "nothing but a witch hunt." (Michaud, 2015)

Of course, there was no actual truth to the idea that Dungeons & Dragons was inspiring children and young adults to adopt satanism or commit violent crimes, yet the fears produced during the panic generated widespread sentiment that something must to done to stop the game from destroying the moral fabric of society. Perhaps you can think of other more recent examples of popular culture and moral panics stoking fear and prompting calls eradicate social problems like mass violence, terrorism, predatory sex crimes, and many other perceived threats to the social welfare.

Blaming

You may have heard the mantra "if it bleeds, it leads," which commonly refers to the notion that news agencies prioritize reporting about acts of violence that elicit fear among audiences. Well, this mantra is not just confined to news; it is a guiding principle in popular entertainment. The depictions of criminal activity and investigation on popular television shows like *CSI: Crime Scene Investigation, Criminal Minds*, and even the more fantastical *Game of Thrones* have become increasingly graphic in recent decades, as have images of crime in films, video games, novels, and comic books (see Rafter, 2006; Deutsch and Cavender, 2008; Phillips and Strobl, 2013). This is an important point because these types of hyper-violent, sensationalized portraits of social life have far-reaching implications.

Opinion polls routinely indicate that most Americans believe crime is worsening despite the fact crime rates have actually been in decline since the early 1990s. Numerous studies have also found that regular viewers of crime news and popular crime shows report greater fear of crime (Callanan, 2012), and are generally more supportive of harsh, punitive punishments (Kort-Butler and Sittner Hartshorn, 2011). Put simply, the vast majority of news and entertainment content offers a view of the world that is couched in shocking tales filled with emotional rhetoric and fear-laden storylines regardless of whether or not the information presented is factually accurate (Altheide, 2002; Doyle, 2003).

With this in mind, let us return to the Isla Vista killings committed by Elliot Rodger. Within the first 24 hours after news of the mass shooting broke – when emotions were high and people were feverishly searching for answers – a number of media figures, politicians, and other claims-makers stridently blamed popular culture. For some, the very shocking nature of the crimes might have seemed to mirror the plot of a television crime drama or a Lifetime movie. Actually, this seeming convergence of real life and entertainment was confirmed a few months later when *Law & Order: Special Victims Unit* aired an episode entitled *Holden's Manifesto*. Clearly inspired by the Elliot Rodger case, the episode focused on investigators' efforts to track a misogynistic sociopath dubbed the "virgin killer." In real life, however, much of the blame for Rodger's crimes was directed toward popular culture. Considerable scorn and moral outrage was focused on video games, partly because Rodger was an ardent *World of Warcraft* player. Take, for example, this on air plea offered by conservative radio host Glenn Beck, as recounted by online journalist Erica Ritz in 2014:

> "Please listen to me. You've got to get the video games out of your child's hands. Please. I'm having a hard enough time trying to do it in my own home. Enough. No more. Because they cannot handle it. This is not the same as Pac-Man. It is not the same. These are virtual worlds where they live. They live in these worlds; talk to them."

Similar claims were made in the weeks following the Sandy Hook school shooting in 2012, when the National Rifle Association's (NRA) executive vice president, Wayne LaPierre, was among those who sought to place the blame on video games and Hollywood movies for cultivating a violent culture in the Unites States (Curry, 2012).

> The truth is that our society is populated by an unknown number of genuine monsters – people so deranged, so evil, so possessed by voices and driven by demons that no sane person can possibly ever comprehend them. They walk among us every day. And here's another dirty little truth that the media try their best to conceal: There exists in this country a callous, corrupt and corrupting shadow industry that sells, and sows,

violence against its own people… Through vicious, violent video games with names like *Bulletstorm*, *Grand Theft Auto*, *Mortal Kombat* and *Splatterhouse*. And here's one: it's called *Kindergarten Killers*. It's been online for 10 years. Then there's the blood-soaked slasher films like *American Psycho* and *Natural Born Killers* that are aired like propaganda loops on *Splatterdays* and every day, and a thousand music videos that portray life as a joke and murder as a way of life. And then they have the nerve to call it entertainment. (San Jose Mercury News, 2012)

LaPierre's public remarks must be understood in context. Many claims-makers framed Sandy Hook as a gun control problem, thus putting the NRA on the defensive from the outset. His comments, which came more than a week after the shooting, reflect what social problems scholars refer to as a *counterclaim*, which is a statement that challenges the message of a previous claim (for example, arguing for gun rights in response to claims advocating gun control). By attributing responsibility to things like video games, movies, and deranged "monsters," LaPierre was seeking to alter public interpretations of this tragedy – shifting it away from a "gun problem" to some other source of blame – while also advancing the NRA's own political agenda. Whatever his motives, LaPierre's comments are illustrative of the many claims presuming a strong and unassailable link between popular culture and violence that tend to circulate in the aftermath of high-profile mass shootings.

It is important to note that while video games have drawn a great deal of scrutiny in recent years for their purported role in promoting violence, blame also gets assigned to all manner of popular culture. This was evidenced after the Isla Vista shootings by the many reporters, pundits, and claimants who noted Elliot Rodger's father was a producer for the popular *The Hunger Games* movies, which feature a heavy dose of both implied and enacted violence amidst a dystopian world marked by fear and brutality. For example, an article published on *The Telegraph* (United Kingdom) website implies Rodger's crimes are connected to a more general "culture of violence" propagated by the mainstream entertainment industry:

His father is famous for helping to make *The Hunger Games*, the futuristic Hollywood blockbuster about teenagers pitted against each other in a fight to the death. However, Elliot Rodger created his own dystopian drama yesterday when he embarked on a deadly rampage, killing six people – just hours after posting a video online declaring war on the comfortable Californian world in which he grew up. (Sherwell, 2014: 32)

In this instance, popular culture is positioned as a sort of co-conspirator in Rodger's spree, associating the crimes to the various connections he and his family had to Hollywood celebrities and the entertainment industry.

Oftentimes popular culture is presented in these sorts of menacing ways, depicted as a corruptive force that can transform people into monsters capable of inflicting considerable evil on others. Take the case of Richard McCroskey, an aspiring young rapper who in 2009 brutally murdered his girlfriend, her parents, and her friend in Farmville, Virginia. Many of the subsequent news reports suggested "music was behind the murders" due to McCroskey's love of Horrorcore, "which sets lyrics of murder, mutilation, and decomposing bodies to hip-hop beats" (Martinez, 2009). Although it was often noted that McCroskey was "a young man with no criminal record," most every news story focused on McCroskey's penchant for rapping "about the thrill of murder" (Associated Press, 2009). In one account he was described as taking "delight in the blend of horror hip-hop that celebrated macabre killings," while noting "in one YouTube video, he holds a hatchet and sings about killing people and putting their remains in black bags: 'Last night I was the murderous rage. Now, I gotta get rid of the bodies before the corpses start to get to rotting'" (Drash, 2009).

Of course, there was no specific evidence linking McCroskey's actions to his taste in music (in much the same way there was no reason to believe Rodger's crimes were connected to *The Hunger Games*). By McCroskey's own admission, music had nothing to do with his decision to kill: "When he was being led to jail, McCroskey told reporters, 'Jesus told me to do it'" (Drash, 2009). It may very well be that McCroskey's declaration of divine intervention speaks to an underlying mental disorder that possibly triggered his violent conduct. In fact, there is evidence to suggest both youth and parental mental health issues more directly correlates with violence and other at-risk behaviors than music, movies, video games, or popular culture more generally (Barnes, 1999; Payton et al, 2000; Monahan et al, 2005). A growing body of research also finds the societal prevalence of misogyny, sexual devaluation of women, exaggerated notions of masculinity, and patriarchy might contribute to why some males commit mass shootings and violent crimes – all themes, it should be noted, that are highly prevalent and commonly depicted in popular culture.

Box 3.2: Slender Man

Slender Man is a fictitious online boogeyman who first emerged in the public consciousness in 2009, and in the years since he has been blamed for murders, violence, and a host of other cultural concerns. There is, of course, a problem with blaming Slender Man for these things: he does not actually exist. As a 2014 profile of the character in *The Washington Post* notes: "Slender Man, perhaps the Internet's best and scariest legend, is indeed a legend – an invented character who can be traced back, quite linearly, to an obscure forum where ... users Photoshopped old pictures and improvised a back story for their creations" (Dewey, 2014). The first online sighting of Slender Man involved two pictures, each featuring a different group of children but with the same tall, faceless man visible in the background. The pictures were carefully put together in a way that made them seem authentic, which helped fuel the impression that something menacing happened to the children in the photo. In the ensuing years, the burgeoning Slender Man urban legend spawned countless additional Photoshopped images as well as fan fiction and YouTube videos depicting the character in various locales. In 2012, a Slender Man video game was released (players are placed in a "virtual" forest with just a flashlight and tasked with retrieving eight pieces of paper before Slender Man finds them), and this helped bring the tale to a new medium and broader audiences.

In the spring of 2014, the tale of Slender Man entered the mainstream news cycle when he was cited directly as the motive for two attempted murders. The first involved a pair of 12-year-old Wisconsin girls who lured a friend into the woods after a sleepover and stabbed her 19 times, allegedly in tribute to Slender Man; the other, a teen in Ohio who attacked her mother as a show of her devotion to Slender Man. The Wisconsin case in particular attracted a great deal of media attention and has been covered by a range of television news magazines and other high-profile media sources, including an HBO documentary scheduled to premiere in 2016. Much of the coverage has sought to explain why two young girls would commit such a horrific crime when they were said to possess many socially valued attributes (eg honor students, caring, kind and so on). These sorts of accounts are important because they further the appeal of blaming. For instance, media depictions suggested that the girls were not simply monsters on a predetermined path toward violence and depravity. Unable to blame some innate characteristics of these "good girls", news narratives shifted away from the girls themselves for some sort of causal explanation.

Enter Slender Man. The key to Slender Man's diffusion into different forms of popular culture and its lasting appeal is that it is a tale that offers – like most urban legends – flexibility in how it gets told. The details of the character's origins and motives are fuzzy and can be adapted in ways that allow it to be told any place at any time, giving it localized details that make it relatable while still hewing to cultural narratives that we all already know and routinely circulate (eg ideas about children being uniquely vulnerable to predatory dangers, or the internet as a breeding ground for all sorts of sin and vice). Slender Man and other urban legends fill a cultural need for explanations of disconcerting phenomena because they are "a metaphor for 'helplessness, power differentials, and anonymous forces.' He's an infinitely morphable stand-in for things we can neither understand nor control, universal fears that can drive people to great lengths – even, it would appear, very scary, cold-blooded lengths" (Dewey, 2014). Even when issues or events are not directly linked to Slender Man, the general belief in his existence can make future reports of nefarious internet characters or predatory strangers seem all the more plausible.

Perhaps it is unsurprising, then, that a 2013 poll conducted by *Vanity Fair* and *60 Minutes* found approximately 80% of respondents believe depictions of violence in popular culture contribute to real-world violence; a mere 6% think movies and video games do not inspire violence (Eggerton, 2013). These results are not only in line with other recent public opinion surveys – including a 2012 Rasmussen Reports poll that similarly found the majority of Americans believe "violent movies and television shows lead to more violence in society" (Rasmussen Reports, 2012) – they are consistent with polling data that date back to the 1950s!

> When a 1999 Gallup poll asked adults whether the depiction of violence in popular entertainment (such as TV, in the movies, music, and video games) was one of the major causes of violence among young people, a majority (62%) said it was. A separate poll from that year found that 74% of Americans thought some of the blame for teen-age crime could be placed on television and movies violence. Thirty-one percent (31%), thought TV and movie violence deserved "a great deal" of the blame. A Gallup poll from 1954 found remarkably similar results. In that survey, 70% of American adults thought blame for teen-age crime could be placed on "mystery and crime programs on TV and radio" – 24% assigned the programs "a great deal" of blame, with another 44% assigning "some" blame. The results were similar for comic books, which were just gaining mainstream popularity in the 1950s. Again, 70% said the reading of comic books could be blamed for teen-age crime, with 26% assigning "a great deal" of blame. (Carlson, 2002)

Although fears over comic books might nowadays seem amusing, at one time there was a movement to ban them, and congressional hearings were even held in response to fears about their supposed influence on juvenile delinquency (US Senate, 1954a; 1954b; Wertham, 1954; Phillips and Strobl, 2013). What's more, pinball machines actually were forbidden in most American cities from the 1940s until 1976, over fears they were gambling devices used to separate hapless victims from their money. Clearly, people have been blaming popular culture for causing social problems like violent crime, gambling, drug abuse, and promiscuity for quite a long time.

With this in mind, it is important to consider the reasons why news workers, elected officials, and citizens are so quick to assign blame when social problems are brought to public attention. Furthermore, why do these efforts so often become focused on popular culture as the cause of the problems? To answer these questions it is necessary to look more closely at how social problems get identified and presented to audiences.

The appeal of blaming

The modern historical landscape is dotted with a seemingly endless collection of examples in which collective fear and presumptions of moral decay have coalesced around popular culture forms. In the early 20th century, for example, radio technology was an object of considerable public distress. Much of this concern was based in the fact that radio allowed people to access news and entertainment programming in real time. At the time, critics argued that allowing people to listen to anything they wanted whenever they wanted could lead to them becoming detached from their moral and spiritual link to the community. Children were said to be particularly vulnerable to unchecked radio programming, based on the belief that they would be swayed toward deviant behaviors through exposure to dangerous, amoral programming (DeFleur, 1966).

By the mid–20th century, concerns continued to emerge about the content flowing over radio and television airwaves. Much of this collective anxiety was itself a product of the persistent drumbeat of fear propagated by a collection of political leaders, religious officials, parental groups, and various other moral entrepreneurs. For instance, in the 1950s parents and religious leaders expressed great concern that Elvis Presley's swiveling hips would send impressionable young women into uncontrolled sexual frenzy. During the 1960s, some citizen groups worried the unprecedented popularity of The Beatles would result in a culture of drug-addled teens because the band was said to be subversively encouraging drug use through their lyrics. Similar concerns about drugs, sexual promiscuity, and even Satanism were also attached to popular rock groups such as Led Zeppelin and Black Sabbath in the 1970s. Furthermore, as hip-hop and rap music gained popularity through the 1980s and 1990s, there was widespread concern and that lyrics of artists like 2 Live Crew and NWA would infect the minds of suburban white youth with values favoring violence, misogyny and disrespect for authority (see Binder, 1993). Later in the 1990s, these anxieties shifted blame toward "shock rockers" like Marilyn Manson for teen problems such as drug use and suicide. The point here is that generalized concerns about popular music being a direct cause of various social ills are a recurring feature of modern life. They never actually go away;

the focus just switches from one artist or genre to another. We can see this today with recent allegations toward Miley Cyrus for glorifying the drug "molly" in her song lyrics and hyper-sexualized public displays. The persistence of these presumptions that a strong causal relationship exists between popular music and various social concerns is remarkable when we consider how much things have changed both in the relatively narrow confines of the music industry and in society in general.

Historical fears directed at radio and popular music are instructive here for several reasons. Firstly, even though they emerged more than a century ago, claims that radio would destroy the moral fabric of society paved the way for many of the regulatory controls that govern popular music, movies, and television today, including movie ratings provided by the Motion Picture Association of America, and the "explicit content" advisory labels affixed to music deemed objectionable. Also, the longstanding success of the politicians and claims-makers in scapegoating popular culture, cultivated a deeply supportive context for the idea that things like music, comic books, movies, video games, online chat rooms and even personal fashion choices are agents of harm. As a result, there are now many people who simply take it on fact that popular culture is *the* smoking gun that must be addressed in order to cure social problems like violent crime.

The blame game starts with a claim

In some ways, the popularity of blaming popular culture may lie in its simplicity – uncomplicated answers to complicated social issues offer more comfort than admitting there is no answer at all. To the extent that media help identify social problems and steer conversations about how to solve them, it stands to reason that the people and groups that help shape mediated messages – from political and corporate leaders to activists and news personalities – have a powerful voice in determining how we interpret and respond to those issues. Politicians, activists, and all sorts of other claims-makers are well aware of how the press operates, so they actively seek to connect with citizens by making themselves publicly visible on issues like violent crime, gun control, and victimization. On a typical day you might not even recognize this process in action, but in those moments when fear is high and people are feeling most vulnerable – perhaps in the aftermath of a particularly heinous crime or a tragic accident – we are suddenly bombarded with seemingly inarguable claims about causes and solutions that will help to "make things right." In most instances what emerges is a sort of "blame game" in which claims-makers focus on a single factor as the reason for the problem and the would-be target for solving the matter.

To truly understand the appeal of blaming in general, and blaming popular culture more specifically, consider the contextual forces that guide and shape our understandings of social problems. Throughout this chapter it has been noted that blaming has rhetorical value for claims-makers because it can influence how people make sense of and attempt to deal with troubling issues. Given advancements in media technology and communications, which offer a previously inconceivable ability to produce and consume information with remarkable speed and efficiency, blaming has seemingly become even more diffuse in public discourse. And this has occurred for good reason. Nowadays there is essentially an unending stream of social problems claims swirling around us at all times. In one sense this is very democratizing because the internet and rise of citizen journalism mean that more people than ever before can make and attempt to broadly disseminate social problems claims. The downside, however, is it can be really hard for any particular claim to stand out amidst all of the other competing claims. Given the overabundance of information availability in modern society, blame is ideal because it is simple, can be mustered up and articulated very quickly, and yields the sort of narrow and evocative sound bites that help claims-makers gain entry into the news cycle. Although blame requires little deep thinking or critical reflection, it provides a readily available means of "out-shouting" or "out-emoting" one's competitors – no small feat in a crowded social problems marketplace where one is always at risk of not being heard among the cacophony of claims.

Social problems scholars have repeatedly shown that those who seek to create concerns around a troubling condition have to meet a few requirements to draw the public attention and social responses that they seek. Some of these efforts are obvious, like giving the problem a name (eg "drunk driving," "road rage," or "sexting"), providing examples of what it looks like (eg the image of predatory strangers stealing kids), offering estimates of just how big the problem is purported to be, and outlining how the problem can be cured (Best, 2013). However, if the goal is to get people to take notice and care about the issue – and maybe even do something in response – then claims-makers must go further. That is, they also have to offer a compelling explanation for *why* the problem exists. This sounds easy enough, but most problems are actually quite complicated and come into existence due to a multitude of factors. Any attempt to address all of the possible causes of a social problem is likely to be so complex to convey and difficult to understand that it would cause public attention to wane before a policy response could be formulated, let alone actually implemented. As a general rule, then, simple explanations are valued. Consequently, many of the claims we receive via mass media offer little more than dramatic and easy-to-understand accounts that are often built upon oversimplified notions of cause-and-effect relationships (ie blame), regardless of whether or not they accurately depict the underlying source(s) of the problem.

The blame game continues with a frame

As claims are communicated to audiences about causes and consequences of various social problems, decisions must be made about what information should be included, emphasized, or altogether excluded from the public discourse. Sociologists refer to this as *framing* and it is intended to influence how audiences perceive and identify with prospective social problems (Jenness, 1995; Benford and Snow, 2000). According to Joel Best (2008), frames encourage "viewing the world from a particular perspective; they give meaning to what otherwise seem confusing, so that once someone adopts a given frame, everything seems to be clearer, to make sense" (2008: 68).

To better understand how framing works, think of someone standing in front of a window. While there is a great big world outside, the only part of it visible to that person is what can be seen through the window. If someone spent their entire life looking through that window, what they saw would shape their understanding of the world. Thus, if they looked out and always saw bright sunshine, they could conclude that the world is full of good weather, notwithstanding the forecast in other areas of the globe not visible through the window might be gloomy and full of rain or something more disastrous like a hurricane. Extending this analogy toward popular culture, imagine if your understanding of the world was shaped solely from movies directed by Michael Bay. You might conclude that you should never leave your home for fear that cars and office buildings are exploding everywhere, and vehicles may suddenly transform into giant robots! Framing, then, is important because it shapes how we receive and interpret all of the social problems brought to our attention.

Quite often, the issues we come to recognize as social problems are framed as some sort of immediate or future threat that we should fear. Consider something as seemingly innocuous as children trick-or-treating for Halloween candy. Every year around October you are likely to see a familiar collection of news reports, public outreach campaigns, and rumors that help to fuse Halloween with real-world fears. In particular, news agencies invariably run stories warning parents about Halloween sadism and the need to inspect their children's sweets to make sure that they are safe to eat. In October, 2015, for example, a story began circulating in the week leading up to Halloween alleging that visitors to a Texas haunted house attraction discovered a deranged man eating a teenaged boy inside the attraction. The story quickly went viral and even was included in broadcast news coverage. These sorts of reports are undoubtedly meant as a public service, and the underlying message to protect children is a valuable one. Yet they ultimately cultivate fear of a non-existent threat. Only five cases of tainted Halloween candy deaths have ever been documented in the United States; none included sadism and the lone criminal incident involved relatives intentionally poisoning a child (see Best and Horiuchi, 1985; Best, 1990; 2015). The story of the Texas haunted house cannibal was also quickly debunked when it was traced to a satirical news website (LaCapria, 2015). If coverage of Halloween sadism and tainted candy tells us anything, it is that assumptions about the link between popular culture and violent crime has become something of ritual and folklore, regenerated from generation to generation and reinforced through continued media notoriety.

Why popular culture is blameworthy

To this point, the blaming of popular culture has been discussed as a valuable rhetorical strategy for claims-makers. But what is it about popular culture that makes it such an easy target for blame? Part of the answer to this question can be found in the very nature of popular culture itself. Many of the most prominent forms of popular culture – films, television, music, video games, comic books, fashion, and so on – are riddled with sex, violence, and drug use, all of which are commonly used by claim-makers to symbolize moral decay. Take, for example, an article published in April of 2014, on the Reverend Billy Graham's website that warned of Hollywood's immoral agenda to "take over society and strike Christian values from the landscape" by glorifying monetary wealth (perhaps ironic given Graham's own personal fortune), the acceptability of profane language and gratuitous sex, and endorsing deviant behaviors.

> We're a far cry from the days of John Wayne, Pat Boone, and *The Brady Bunch.* Instead of wholesome family values, today's secular offerings smack of smut, including network television series openly promoting homosexuality and polygamy… Modern culture didn't get here overnight … it's been a gradual decline. (Chandler, 2014)

The solution, according to Graham's ministry, is "to loosen the stronghold Hollywood has on culture" by demanding entertainment options that eschews violence, sexuality, and alternative lifestyle choices, which represent an "all out assault on the traditional family." (Chandler, 2014). Of course, crime, violence, and gratuitous sexuality all existed long before the advent of modern popular culture, yet focusing the blame on popular culture remains effective because of its simplicity. It is simply easier for claimants to suggest the bogeyman can be located in all manner of entertainment than it is to develop a nuanced long-term plan for addressing mental illness, access to lethal weaponry, structural inequality, or any of the other complex factors that may hold predictive or explanatory value when it comes to violence and other social concerns.

The fact of the matter is, claims about popular culture being the cause of societal problems are easy to "sell" because they pique the interests of news organizations and resonate with the citizenry. Yet popular culture, offers claims-makers a number of additional advantages when fashioning their blame claims. Firstly, the sheer breadth and reach of popular culture means that there is an almost limitless assortment of potential targets for blame. Second, popular culture is intertwined with our daily lives in so many deep and intricate ways that claims can take on a heightened sense of relevance among audiences. Third, the popular culture industry constantly produces new and exciting things to consume, making it uniquely amenable to blame claims assigning it harm. New technologies, for instance, are often said to be destroying interpersonal communication as more and more people interact in virtual environments that facilitate cyberbullying, sexting, pedophilia, sex trafficking, and a host of other emerging concerns. This creates a context in which it is really easy to focus all of the blame on a simple piece of technology while ignoring the many other factors that might also help explain these worrisome issues.

Certainly much of the blame that popular culture receives for producing social ills is rooted in the persistent collective belief that things are always changing for the worse. If you have ever heard an older family member talking about how music and movies were better in the old days when people were more respectful, then you likely understand the tendency to believe things used to be better, even though the not too distant past was filled with unspeakable atrocities like slavery, legal segregation, genocide, and the Holocaust. The paradox, though, is that 100 years ago people were making similar claims about how society was falling apart at the seams. In the early 20th century, for example, women at beaches in the United States were subject to inspection and could receive a fine if their bathing suits displayed too much leg, even though swimwear was far less revealing than what is commonly seen today. The point is that fads and fashions of popular culture continue to evolve and change, but lingering fears that pop culture is harming society tend to reproduce themselves from one generation to the next.

Do we have to play the blame game?

As this chapter has attempted to demonstrate, blaming popular culture for social problems is not a recent phenomenon. However, examining the matter using a critical, scholarly lens exposes blaming as a deeply flawed approach to understanding social problems. Most often, blame reflects a knee-jerk emotional response but offers relatively little productive value. Yet, for claims-makers, there is tremendous value to employing blame as a rhetorical strategy for advancing claims within a crowded social problems marketplace. We may reasonably assume that those who look to quickly blame popular culture for a social problem are obfuscating, misdirecting, or deliberately spreading falsehoods when they utter embellished statements about social problems and their preferred solutions. Yet such a conclusion would oversimplify things because the effectiveness of blaming popular culture for the existence of social problems resides in the fact that it is not entirely removed from the truth. Movies, television shows, music, and many other elements of pop culture that people consume every singe day are in fact riddled with violence, overt sexuality, and many other presumed vices that are commonly associated with a variety of societal ills.

Claims-makers are merely connecting the dots by realizing the value of playing the blame game. News outlets, after all, respond to dramatic, engaging, simplistic, and even hyperbolic claims about social problems, particularly when they piggyback on newsworthy events like a school shooting or an act of "random" crime. Blame, therefore, helps claims get labeled as problematic "in the arenas of public discourse and action" by framing them in a way that facilitates heightened news awareness and piques audience interest (see Hilgartner and Bosk, 1988: 70). And since the goal of claims making is to get your message heard, it really does not matter to claimants whether their declarations are factually accurate or truthful, so long as they sway public opinion and influence policymaking. The rhetorical value of blame renders moot the fact that there is scant definitive empirical evidence connecting popular culture to aggressive behavior and real-life violence or virtually any other social problem (Freedman, 2002; Trend, 2007). These explanations remain popular among the general public, pundits, and public officials not because they are necessarily true, but because they are a great way to gain traction in an intensely competitive public sphere that values entertainment and sensationalism above all else.

It might very well be that some forms of popular culture are indeed harmful, so researchers should continue to examine possible correlations between pop culture and various social problems. But in our roles as both recipients of social problems claims and participants in popular culture we must remain critical of the blame game. Our social world is incredibly complicated. Claims that reduce complex social phenomena into a simplistic cause-and-effect narrative should always be met with skepticism. While the search for the *smoking gun* – that single factor that promises to reveal the cause and solution to our most pressing social concerns – is understandable, it is in many ways a fool's errand. Social problems take shape through the complex interplay of individual, structural, and cultural forces. Consequently, the means of effectively addressing them are likely to be found amidst our social institutions and political processes when spurred by an engaged and informed citizenry, and not by demonizing movies, music, clothing styles, tattoos, and other innocuous non-conformist behaviors inspired by pop culture.

Popular culture ultimately has the power to both liberate and control, meaning it can help free us from the scourge of social problems like racism, sexism, homophobia, and inequality, while simultaneously proliferating messages that reinforce and perpetuate those very same harms. Getting too caught up in playing the blame game prevents society from identifying all of the ways that popular culture can be employed as a mechanism for spreading awareness and meaningfully addressing social problems. At the same time, if we rely too much on popular culture to lead the fight for change, then we run the risk of becoming even more subject to the power of a corporatized culture industry that uses entertainment and leisure to manipulate "the needs of consumers – producing, controlling, disciplining them" (Horkheimer and Adorno, [1944] 2002: 115). If there is one lesson to be learned, it is that pop culture should be viewed with a healthy dose of skepticism, while understanding that the problems we face in society are far too complex to be explained by simply blaming movies, music, or any other form of recreation we choose to consume.

KEY QUESTIONS

What are media frenzies? How and why do they influence the use of blaming as a claims-making strategy?

What is the "blame game" and how does it affect how we understand and respond to social problems?

Why is directing blame toward various forms of popular culture so appealing to claims-makers?

SUGGESTED READINGS

Berry, J.M. and Sobieraj. S. (2014) *The outrage industry: Political opinion, media and the new incivility*, Oxford: Oxford University Press.

Furedi, F. (2006) *Culture of fear revisited: Risk-taking and the morality of low expectation*, London: Bloomsbury.

Maratea, R.J. and Monahan, B.A. (2013) "Crime control as mediated spectacle: the institutionalization of gonzo rhetoric in modern media and politics", *Symbolic Interaction* 36: 261-74.

FOUR

Spreading Problem Claims Through Popular Culture

Y ou may recall the horrifying hours following the 2013 Boston Marathon bombing, when news agencies were scrambling to quickly distribute as much information as possible to the public about the attack, its perpetrators, the victims, and the ensuing police manhunt. Faced with considerable pressure to update audiences on the latest developments and out-scoop journalistic competitors, CNN's John King reported "a significant development" in the ongoing investigation when claimed on air and via Twitter that authorities had identified a "dark-skinned" male suspect (see CNN, 2013). The problem, however, is that King's "scoop" was wrong and federal authorities quickly denounced the report by stating on record that no arrest had been made (Wemple, 2013). The actual suspects, Dzhokhar and Tamerlan Tsarnaev would not be formally identified until more than 24 hours later.

By that time, King's scoop had long since taken hold of the coverage cycle. Cable news networks were awash with surveillance footage purporting to show suspicious "dark-skinned" men lurking among the unsuspecting crowd as they hatched their deadly terrorist plot. In Boston, a local NBC affiliate aired a report showing photos of a man running away from the carnage, while the reporter asked if he was somehow associated with the attack (Amira, 2013). Fox News reporters focused for a time on a Saudi Arabian man injured during the bombings and repeatedly questioned whether he was the perpetrator, even though he was never declared a suspect by law enforcement. A remarkably similar scenario was simultaneously unfolding online, where cyber vigilantes and virtual lynch mobs targeted any male they could identify at the scene with dark-colored skin and "terrorist-sounding" names.

If there is an important lesson to be learned from this example of how King's erroneous news "scoop" directly influenced social responses to the Boston Marathon bombing, it is that the power to disseminate information to large audiences in the public sphere is a significant advantage in the social problems process. Claims that circulate through mass media can have a profound effect on individual and collective perceptions regardless of whether that information is accurate, correct, or truthful. So why is this important as it relates to social problems? Imagine you are a claims-maker or an activist attempting to convince the public about how they should respond to a social problem like domestic terrorism. You will probably recognize that if you are going to be successful in this task it is important to have your claims circulated to the large public through mass media and popular culture, particularly on television, radio, in newspapers and magazines, and online. Because, as the John King example indicates, if your claims are received by audiences, then you as a claimant have the opportunity to both shape the narrative in a way that promotes your agenda and manipulate public perceptions regardless of whether the claims you disseminate are factually truthful or deliberately dishonest. Claims-making, then, is not about being honest and objectively defending the public good; it is about the power to be heard in the public sphere and how that power influences public perceptions about social problems.

Box 4.1: British Petroleum and the 2010 Gulf of Mexico oil spill

For 87 days during the spring and summer of 2010, the Deepwater Horizon oil spill discharged approximately 210 million gallons (US) into the Gulf of Mexico, and devastated wetlands and wildlife across Louisiana and the southern Gulf coast of the United States. With the oil still gushing and media attention shifted toward the emergent environmental disaster, a press conference was held by Tony Hayward, CEO of British Petroleum (BP), the company whose rig exploded, thereby producing the spill. As news outlets transmitted his words across the globe, Hayward mitigated both the effects of the disaster and his own company's liability, as well as offering solutions for solving the problem by "capping" the leaking well. In these highly publicized moments, Hayward was generating claims with the intent of persuading audiences that his company had limited culpability in the disaster, while also propagandizing about the safety of oil drilling, minimal ecological harm caused by oil spills, and the social conscience of everyone at British Petroleum (a victim, per Hayward) whose primary goal was to help solve the problem.

Hayward's claims were soon splashed across newspaper headlines and websites, while pundits debated the merit of his words during television newscasts, talk radio programs, and even podcasts. Yet BP's efforts to manipulate public opinion did not stop there. The company also used its considerable financial clout to manipulate search engines like Google and Yahoo!, so that people seeking to learn more about the spill would find information sympathetic to BP and the oil industry, more generally.

> BP, the very company responsible for the oil spill that is already the worst in US history, has purchased several phrases on search engines such as Google and Yahoo so that the first result that shows up directs information seekers to the company's official website. A simple Google search of "oil spill" turns up several thousand news results, but the first link, highlighted at the very top of the page, is from BP. "Learn more about how BP is helping," the link's tagline reads. (Friedman, 2010)

By maximizing the tremendous institutional and economic power of a multinational corporation, executives at BP deliberately used popular culture to try and control the flow of information reaching audiences about the oil spill. In many ways the company's public relations efforts were successful. Despite widespread public anger following the spill, BP resumed drilling operations in the Gulf of Mexico a little more than a year later.

Spreading

Social problems scholars often suggest that anyone can participate in the claims-making process, and this is no doubt technically correct. Two people in a coffee shop discussing current events are likely to express claims to one another, and perhaps be overheard by those sitting near them. A person on a street corner holding a sign for passersby to read is expressing a claim. However, their relative social voice is limited because they lack sufficient notoriety, credibility, and authority to command media and public attention, meaning their claims are unlikely to resonate beyond their immediate friends and family. Social power, then, plays an important role in distinguishing successful from unsuccessful claims-making, because it helps establish and legitimize claimants' relevance in the public sphere, within which popular culture influences the nature and scope of information we consume in everyday life. In this sense, popular culture is more than just a target for blame in the social problems game; it is also a resource that can be used by claims-makers to shape and/or deliver meanings to audiences, often in ways that can make these messages seem more relatable. This can have profound consequences because it allows those people and groups with sufficient social power to greatly shape – if not outright control – the messages about social problems and bring them into alignment with their preferred solutions.

If we think about social problems as having a lifespan – a beginning when the problem is recognized; a middle when the problem is debated; and an end when the issue is solved or, at least, ceases to be viewed as a relevant concern – then it becomes easier to visualize (1) how popular culture helps spread and institutionalize social problems, and (2) why those people and groups with the authority to influence the content and flow of publicly available information have considerable power in shaping our thoughts about social problems and their solutions. More importantly, this fusion of popular culture with social problems claims making tends to *prioritize bureaucratic accounts*, thus expanding the capacity to shape social narratives among claimants possessing institutional power in the public sphere. In other words, the claims-making efforts of public officials, political leaders, business moguls, and media figures are positioned advantageously above those made by fledgling activists and lay citizens, and are therefore more likely to shape media discourse and influence public perceptions of social problems.

From this perspective, popular culture functions as a lens whereby our collective focus is directed towards the views of various social problems endorsed by powerful institutional and bureaucratic *insiders* who have the social power needed to command the attention of news workers and policymakers. In contrast, activists and other citizen *outsiders* who lack name recognition and sufficient economic resources typically (but not always) have trouble getting their claims recognized by the public. This point highlights how and why having social power in the public sphere gives claimants greater ability to *spread* claims about social problems through popular culture and deliver them to expansive audiences. It is important to keep in mind that popular culture encompasses all manners of *everyday life and mass consumerism*, which means its role in our lives is shaped by those who control the political and commercial fads and fashions – from clothing and iPhones, to television shows and tabloid gossip – that reverberate through society at any given time. The point is that celebrities, business leaders, policymakers, and other social elites are granted access to news cycles because they pique audience interest by identifying relevant trends, interesting gossip and information (including claims about social problems), and trendy consumer products. From a social problems perspective it is understandable why the claims made by these sorts of people and groups are valuable commodities: Their public visibility lends credibility to the existence and severity of social problems, as well as the media reports that chronicle them; and when funneled through popular culture, their claims may find new and bigger audiences. As importantly, when social problem advocacy is filtered through the lens of popular culture, the messages and claims that reach the public oftentimes look a lot more like entertainment than activism.

Spreading adds another layer to our understanding of the linkages between social problems and popular culture because it reinforces that popular culture is not simply a benign vehicle for transmitting claims about the existence of social problems and how to correct them. It is a powerful coercive force that shapes our individual thoughts, behaviors, and compels people to conform to the dominant cultural understandings about how the world functions (see Marcuse, [1964] 1991). In other words, popular culture is a mechanism for social control that constantly reminds us of the proper and valued ways to act, dress, think, behave, and consume in everyday life. Of course, culture is not static – what is socially repugnant at one point in time may become the norm in the future, and vice versa. These shifting definitions do not simply emerge out of thin air; they are generally the product of committed claims-makers, public officials, and activists, often by using popular culture as a catalyst for getting their message heard.

The key is to understand that when it comes to the social problems process, the ability to to successfully publicize claims is undoubtedly influenced by access to traditional sources of communication power (ie the press and political or corporate insiders). Thus, lobbyists, activists, and political officials often have a tremendous advantage when trying to have their claims heard, while the rest of us have most of our views about social issues – that is, if we even choose to express them – limited to our immediate circle of friends and acquaintances or our social media networks. Even if we wanted to influence popular perceptions about a social problem, we tend to lack the public recognition needed for the powers that be to pay much attention to what we are publishing online. Now imagine how different your experience might be if you were a public official, corporate spokesperson, or member of an influential activist group, like the NRA. Your cultural clout and perceived expertise on social matters would increase the likelihood journalists will interview you and seek your opinion; and when they do, your claims will then be visible in news media, thereby cementing your status as a credible public voice about particular social problems (see van Dijk, 1996).

Propagandizing popular culture

In thinking about spreading, and how it shapes our understanding of social problems, it can be helpful to think of it as a sort of pop culture-themed form of *propaganda*. Propaganda is defined as information used to promote or publicize a particular political cause or point of view. Typically, the term is used to reference clear and obvious attempts by political or media authorities to shape and deliver a message to the public that affirms their ideologies and desired social actions. The idea that popular culture can be a valuable tool for communicating propagandized messages is not all that far-fetched. After all, the most effective propaganda persuades audiences through carefully crafted rhetoric and imagery without them realizing their thoughts and beliefs are being manipulated. This is precisely why "Uncle Sam" and "Rosie the Riveter," two of the most well-known propaganda poster characters in US history, rely on cartoon-like imagery to deliver their messages about support for military action and the need for heightened worker morale, respectively. It is also why governments at times produce films like *Reefer Madness*, which are intended to relay a specific social message under the guise of entertainment.

Reefer Madness poster

© The Strong: http://www.museumofplay.org/online-collections/5/14/93.742

Released back in the 1930s, *Reefer Madness* sought to exploit the public's fascination with moving pictures in order to offer parents and children a cautionary tale about the dangers of marijuana usage. In the movie, the lives of innocent teenagers are destroyed after being persuaded by drug dealers to smoke pot. The moral of the story was to abide by the law and avoid using illegal narcotics.

Celebrity spokespersons

Another way we can see popular culture utilized as a way to spread dominant definitions associated with a particular social problem is in the use of celebrity spokespersons who endorse political candidates or take public stands on social problems like discrimination, drug legalization, and human rights violations. In September of 2015, for example, New

England Patriots quarterback Tom Brady received so much media coverage after offhandedly remarking it would be "great" if Donald Trump became President, he had to publicly pronounce weeks later that "he doesn't yet know who he'll vote for in the 2016 presidential election" (Diamond, 2015). The point is, even though Brady's status as a football player lends him no evident expertise on political matters, his visibility in popular culture and status as an admired celebrity make his endorsement a valued commodity for political candidates.

Box 4.2: First Ladies as insider claims-makers

The role of First Lady of the United States is not an official job, but it is one that is often celebrated and viewed with great seriousness. Throughout history, most First Ladies have focused on particular social problems and devoted a great deal of time and resources to promoting public awareness of those issues. Dolly Madison (1809–17) was a well-known supporter of charities devoted to poor children and orphans. Eleanor Harding (1921–23) was a staunch advocate for animal welfare. Eleanor Roosevelt (1933–45) focused on civil rights and other humanitarian issues. Nancy Reagan (1981–89) spearheaded the "Just Say No" anti-drug campaign. Hillary Clinton (1993–2001) focused extensively on issues related to health care reform. Michelle Obama (2009–16) has targeted childhood obesity and other social causes.

Those who have held this role during the media age have increasingly come to recognize the power of popular culture for communicating messages directly to the public. For instance, the last four First Ladies (Barbara Bush, Hillary Clinton, Laura Bush, and Michelle Obama) have all appeared on *Sesame Street* to spread messages about the virtues of reading or exercise to children and their parents. Betty Ford guest starred on the *Mary Tyler Moore* show in 1976; and most recently, Michelle Obama has been dubbed "the First Lady of Television" by media analysts and political pundits as a result of her more than 50 appearances on various talk shows, sitcoms, and scripted television dramas since her husband took office in 2009.

First Ladies, by virtue of their deep connections to the President and his administration, are able to serve as important claims-makers for their selected issues. Incorporating their claims into popular culture allows them to move away from the more solemn tone typically associated with their role, in favor of fun and humorous messages. For instance, when Michelle Obama wanted to promote the virtues of exercise and healthy eating – as part of her "Let's Move" campaign to combat obesity – she did so by dancing with Jimmy Fallon on *The Tonight Show*, engaging in a push-up contest with Ellen DeGeneres on *Ellen*, exercising with contestants on *The Biggest Loser*, and hanging out with the teen stars of Nickelodeon's *iCarly*. Using popular culture in this way helps their claims reach a broader public that includes those who may not closely follow politics. Moreover, many of the scripted shows create storylines that are built around the First Ladies' social causes, giving them a lengthy opportunity to share their claims in an entertaining and engaging way. Celebrities, after all, have the requisite public visibility and notoriety to excite supporters, bring visibility to key issues, and legitimize a social problem (Street, 2002). Although famous people may lack the proficiency of a scholarly or scientific expert, they often have a more powerful sway over public opinion because they have attained a measure of credibility among audiences who recognize them and admire their status (Klapp, 1964). When celebrities advocate for particular social problems, their status within popular culture allows them to legitimize those causes by giving them public exposure that may help attract media attention, while simultaneously increasing the possibility that issues will stand out as important among the general public (Meyer and Gamson, 1995; Street, 2002; Brubaker, 2008). Furthermore, since celebrities "can effectively promote ... more consumer awareness of products and favorable attitudes toward the products they endorse" (Brown, 2003: 44), their presence as spokespersons helps advertise the work of claims-makers and the social problems they seek to cure, thus serving to extend the reach of institutional accounts and reinforcing the problem claims contained therein.

Waging the war on drugs

When celebrities and other public figures filter social problems claims through the lens of popular culture, the narratives that reach the public oftentimes look a lot more like entertainment than activism. We see this in action when popular television programs have, on occasion, broadcast "special episodes" with storylines that focus on controversial social problems like violent crime, sexual assault, child molestation, drug use and so on. One of the more famous instances of a special episode occurred when then First Lady Nancy Reagan appeared on the popular comedy *Diff'rent Strokes* in 1983, to not so subtly advocate for her "Just Say No" anti-drug campaign. During the episode, Reagan asks a classroom full of grammar school students whether they had ever "done a little experimenting" with drugs. Astonished that several of the children responded in the affirmative, mortified adult characters conclude they had been "closing [their] eyes to something [they] didn't want to see," and that all parents and law enforcement should be aware of drug abuse among American youth. In the end, Reagan tells the students (and audiences alike) that she knew "they won't forget any of the things" they learned about the dangers of drugs. Not unlike the previously discussed propaganda film *Reefer Madness*, the episode confronted audiences with a very powerful social message about the importance of conformity to mainstream rules, norms, and moral standards, masked behind a veneer of humor and entertainment.

The *Diff'rent Strokes* example admittedly might seem a bit dated to younger readers, but it is useful to our understanding that the power to use popular culture as a vehicle for social problem claims making has consequences. Decades later, we know the "Just Say No" campaign was one catalyst of the War on Drugs that has had devastating social and economic consequences in the United States. The discriminatory application of drug enforcement has led to the disproportionately harsh arrest and sentencing rates of African-American and Latino offenders, many of whom are denied important social services like food stamps, following a drug crime conviction. All the while, American taxpayer money has been funneled into a prison system that now houses more inmates than any other nation in the world, most of whom are incarcerated for non-violent crimes like marijuana possession, all while tearing apart families and denying many inmates the proper treatment to overcome their drug addictions.

It has only been in recent years that public sentiment has begun to shift in opposition to the War on Drugs and its associated harsh criminal sanctions, which an increasing number of experts, policymakers, and citizens now argue are themselves social problems. Yet for three decades, the War on Drugs persisted with widespread social compliance despite ample evidence of its perilous social costs dating all the way back to the 1980s. At least some, and perhaps most, of the social acceptance of these punitive anti-drug policies was reinforced by repetitious ideological reinforcement about the harms of illegal narcotics found in popular cultural messages. Whether it was the "Just Say No" campaign, movies depicting the seedy and hyper-violent worlds of drug dealers like Nino Brown in *New Jack City*, or songs that relayed messages about the dangers of drug addiction, like *White Lines (Don't Do It)* by Grandmaster Flash and Melle Mel, entertainment media confronted both younger and adult audiences alike with competing messages about the fascinating yet deadly world of drug smuggling and abuse. With the rise of hip-hop culture during the 1990s, many of these same messages continued to find receptive audiences, particularly as the east and west coast street hip-hop and rap, and urban themed movies like *Boyz n the Hood* depicted the violent lives of young African-American men and street gangs in inner cities. All of these genres and themes fueled activists and public officials to perpetuate claims that harsh criminal sanctions for drug dealers and users were the solution to out-of-control black thugs who threatened the welfare of hard-working, mostly white Americans.

The paradox is that many of these popular culture references that exemplified social fears about drug abuse and young black men were actually intended to inspire youth away from dope and to expose society to the harsh reality of life in disenfranchised inner city neighborhoods in American society. Yet the words and imagery of inner city violence, drug abuse, and unsavory fashion styles associated with urban black youth also cultivates fear among a large portion of the population. When these fears are diffused widely via media coverage and co-opted by claims-makers, proclaiming that the solution is to lock up the bad guys and throw away the key, then pop culture often becomes a rallying cry for social order, because it resonates most strongly as a mechanism for bureaucratic social control. The danger, of course, is these messages of compliance to governmental or corporate authority have spread through cultural formats that are designed for popular consumption and are often framed for general entertainment, meaning we tend to absorb them in moments when our guard might be down and we might not be thinking critically.

Promoting patriotism

What's more, efforts to spread social problem claims through popular culture are often targeted toward younger audiences who are particularly susceptible to ideological manipulation. During World War II, for example, comic books targeted children using flamboyant super heroes like Captain America, a "super-soldier created by the US Government" (Dittmer, 2012: 7), who exemplified all-American values of loyalty, bravery, and nationalism fighting alongside military troops. Super heroes also reflect the idyllic moral compass of law-abiding citizens by espousing the values that embody what it means to be a loyal American, such as respect for authority and an ardent sense of patriotism. One of the things that can make something like comic books such a valuable vehicle for spreading meanings is that they are able to couch powerful nationalist sentiment within a leisure activity designed to and entice the audience to consume more.

It is not uncommon to see similar symbolism during sporting events in the United States, where, for example, National Football League (NFL) teams often display American flags as large as the playing field when the national anthem is played before games. Of course, the NFL and other sports leagues have been collectively paid more almost $7 million by the Defense Department and Pentagon to perform these displays of patriotism.

> According to a joint oversight report released by Arizona Republican Sens. John Flake and John McCain on Wednesday. The senators found that since 2012, the Pentagon has signed 72 contracts with teams in the National Football League, Major League Baseball, the National Hockey League, and Major League Soccer that amounted to "paid patriotism." For example, taxpayers paid $49,000 to the Milwaukee Brewers to allow the Wisconsin Army National Guard to sponsor the Sunday singing of "God bless America." In another contract, the New York Jets were paid $20,000 to "recognize one to two New Jersey Army National Guard soldiers as hometown heroes." (Peralta, 2015)

Perhaps more than anything else, *paid* patriotism shows that the cost (and stakes) of truly successful claims-making is high and beyond the reach of most activists with limited financial resources. Both the Defense Department and Pentagon have the money, clout, and social power to manipulate public perceptions by steering the flow of imagery and information in order to "reach a large number of people to connect with the American public" while symbolically and materially promoting their agendas (see Isidore, 2015).

It is indeed unlikely that any of us could similarly compel the NFL to display subversive claims during games even if we had $7 million at our disposal; and chances are, you will never see a Juggalo singing the national anthem or "Autoerotic Asphyxiation Day" at your local ballparks, because the message or claims being made would not resonate positively with large portions of the public in the same way as overarching displays of patriotism. War, of course, is ugly business, and instances of paid patriotism, or commercials advertising discounts for military veterans as thanks for "protecting our way of life" provide blanket praise for whatever military actions the government chooses to take, and masks the reality that American forces sometimes engage in questionable acts of aggression, like the invasion of a sovereign Iraq following 9/11, the Mai Lai massacre during the Vietnam War, and when President Bill Clinton authorized the bombing of a Sudanese pharmaceutical factory in 1998. The point is that the Defense Department and Pentagon are bureaucratic authorities with immense institutional claims-making power to define what is normatively proper – in this case, using claims about heroic troops to coerce blind acceptance of war efforts – while disregarding narratives that undermine the intended message, including instances of atrocities and the failure to provide those same heroic troops with adequate social services after they return from combat.

None of this is to say that every citizen accepts pro-war claims as fact, or that we should collectively avoid patriotic messages and stop supporting military troops. Rather, the messages and claims we receive through mainstream and popular culture about war and the military are largely the product of governmental agencies and bureaucratic actors framing those issues in ways that best promote their interests. The intended purpose of these claims is to promote compliance to the social order and stands in contrast to less influential anti-war protesters who want to convince you to oppose military action. The point is that you should support or oppose military efforts as you see fit, but regardless of your perspective, there are claims-making forces whose job it is to convince to you to align with their perspectives on issues like war, patriotism, and most any other matter of social importance.

Box 4.3: Spreading patriotism through popular culture after 9/11

On September 11, 2001, terrorists hijacked four commercial aircraft, crashing two into New York City's World Trade Center towers, one into the Pentagon in Washington, DC and another in a field in Shanksville, Pennsylvania. The attacks and their aftermath quickly became a "media event" and were covered by national news networks for several days without interruption. Major television networks offered around-the-clock coverage of the attacks and their aftermath, even foregoing commercials in the first few days of that coverage. While news coverage led the way in the first few days after the attacks, popular culture played a vital, if less heralded, role in how the nation engaged with and processed the collective trauma of these events. Concerts, sporting events and even television shows were praised by many as important symbolic reflections of the "American spirit" that would help a wounded nation begin to heal.

In addition to its contributions to collective healing, popular culture also helped to create a supportive context for dramatically altered domestic policies (eg The Patriot Act) as well as the extended military engagements in Iraq and Afghanistan, which would come to define the post-9/11 period in American history. According to Stacy Takacs, "Producers and personalities from the film, television, radio, advertising, and video-gaming industries helped legitimate the War on Terrorism by translating war into entertainment" (2012: 5-6). Eventually, the all-news-all-the-time broadcast cycle ended and commercial programs returned to the airwaves. Many television shows directly or indirectly referenced 9/11 or the "War on Terror". With these shows also came an array of new commercial advertisements that served as patriotic-themed public service campaigns that guided the public toward a collective sense of recovery and resolve. Numerous popular products, such as cars, clothing, and home goods, were assigned virtuous, pro-America meanings as manufacturers and retailers echoed President Bush's declaration that merely "buying things" was patriotic. As Takacs (2012) notes, "By exercising their 'freedom to consume,' the logic went, US citizens would demonstrate the nation's resilience, advertise the American Dream, and help rebuild the nation's economy, thereby defeating the terrorists on a number of fronts" (2012: 7). Video game manufacturers deepened their existing collaborations with the military, resulting in a spate of new ultra-realistic war-themed games, some of which were created expressly to bolster recruitment and promote greater morale among troops in the field. Radio industry leaders helped to streamline and strengthen the pro-war narrative by offering more airplay to some songs (eg those advancing themes of heroism, sacrifice and love for country) and not playing songs deemed "inappropriate" or otherwise not suitable to the post-9/11 spirit that political leaders sought to cultivate (see Monahan, 2010).

Reinforcing gender stereotypes

In many ways, we are all socialized throughout life to comply with the status quo, and popular culture routinely reaffirms for the public how to properly dress, act, behave, and more generally conform to the accepted and desirable cultural mores. Jewelry advertisements, for example, always depict *men and women* in committed and loving monogamous relationships; and commercials for sexual performance medications like Viagra and Cialis represent human sexuality as being hetero-normative. The same rules apply to just about every other advertised product, from household detergents that portray women as responsible for maintaining family hygiene to Burger King using an open-mouthed female model and fellatio analogy ("It'll blow your mind away") to sell its "seven incher" hamburger. In each case the underlying message being relayed through popular culture is one that reinforces the value of conforming to mainstream values as we engage with cultural trends and consume material goods.

To clarify what this means, let us examine the matter of gender norms more closely − in particular the historical and contemporary prevalence in popular culture of framing femininity is an inferior quality that should be restricted to women (see Russo, 1987). Back in the days of silent film, it was relatively common for comedic male actors to either impersonate females or portray stereotypical weaklings forced to confront larger, more masculine bullies in hopes of winning the affection of an attractive female. In doing so, these depictions reinforced traditional gender roles by mocking overly feminine males while reflecting the larger cultural ethos that "a real man was absolute and unyielding" (Russo, 1987: 17, see also Benshoff and Griffin, 2006). Nearly a century later, the portrayal of gender is far less caricaturized, with shows like *Game of Thrones* portraying strong female characters in positions of leadership and authority; and programs like *Glee*, *Transparent*, and *Looking* are all blurring the lines of gender normativity through androgynous depictions of men and women. You might also recall the intense public and political backlash that ensued when J. Crew ran an advertisement depicting a mother painting the color pink on her young son's toenails; and the supportive social response to McKenna Pope, the 13-year-old, who in 2012 delivered a petition with 44,000 signatures to Hasbro, and compelled the toy manufacturer to begin producing its Easy-Bake Oven in gender-neutral colors like black and silver.

At the same time, we can see the persistent and ongoing depictions of stereotypical gender roles and valued masculinity throughout popular culture. Television commercials for household products typically feature a female who is responsible for cleaning the home and feeding her breadwinner husband and young children. Likewise, films like *Here Comes the Boom* and *I Love You, Beth Cooper* routinely portray meek male characters as discovering newfound masculinity in order to triumph in the face of adversity. In both movies the protagonists are at first too feeble to win the affection of a desired female, and reflect the stereotypical presentation of effeminate men as *sissies*. In *I Love You, Beth Cooper*, the brainy nerd, Dennis Cooverman, boldly confesses his love for classmate Beth Cooper – while also pleading for his best friend to admit he is homosexual – during his valedictorian speech. Over the course of the film, he manages to win her heart by participating in a variety of hijinks, which includes confronting her soldier boyfriend, thereby exhibiting "an impossibly pure masculine drive" that allows him to overcome his otherwise damning "feminine behavior and inferiority" (Russo, 1987: 17). Likewise, in *Here Comes the Boom* an otherwise indiscernible teacher played by Kevin James undergoes a radical masculine transformation by becoming a mixed martial arts fighter in order to save his school's music program and earn the adoration of a beautiful female colleague. Television shows like *The Walking Dead* similarly tend to depict even the strongest and most independent of female characters as being in constant need of male supervision, guidance, and protection.

Central to these popular cultural representations is the underlying message that femininity is an inferior and undesirable quality (see Russo, 1987). Male characters, therefore, often reflect a sort of manly rugged individualism, whether they are fighting bad guys, heroically saving the day in disasters films like *San Andreas*, acting as criminal masterminds like Tony Montana in *Scarface*, or even stubbornly attempting to perform surgery on themselves – and meeting their demise in the process – like Dr John Thackery in *The Knick*. These gendered presentations in popular culture also sometimes hint at the dangers of skirting or altogether violating gender norms, like when an overly masculine character in the film *Boys Don't Cry* prompts tragic consequences – including her own sexual and physical assault. They also perpetuate an underlying devaluation of femininity while espousing the message that society functions most effectively when we maintain the patriarchal status quo abiding by expected *heterosexual* gender roles, whereby women are passive, domesticated and feminine, while men remain rugged and ceaselessly masculine.

The messages often emerging through popular culture demand conformity to the hetero-normative mores of American society or risk being seen as a deviant outcast. Contemporary audiences might recognize the scene from the movie *Grease*, when Kenickie asks his T-Birds compatriot Danny Zuko to participate with him in a car race. They instinctively embrace after Zuko agrees, only to realize their other male friends are looking on quizzically, leading both to quickly push away from each other and exhibit exaggerated machismo in frantic attempts to restore their manhood. These sorts of misogynistic portrayals inherently promote the value of manliness over femininity and reassert the value of heterosexuality, while also reflecting the social construction of gender normativity in popular culture.

Conclusion

Oftentimes the difference between a short-lived concern and one with "staying power" is the ability for claimants to continually reassert its relevance and severity in the minds of the public. Popular culture offers an expansive set of tools for not only crafting claims but also for delivering them to broad and diverse audiences over an extended period of time. This makes popular culture quite valuable for claims-makers because it provides new avenues for publicizing their efforts and offers a compelling set of images and narratives that, even though many are fictional in nature, help to cement the dominant definitions associated with the profiled problems. Most importantly, many popular culture products prioritize bureaucratic accounts, which affords those who already tend to have a great deal of the power in the social problems process – political leaders, business moguls, and lobbyists – an additional set of resources to shape problem definitions in ways consistent with their interests. These issues are compounded with certain problems – such as crime – that are commonly featured in television, film and other forms of popular culture. What results is a communication system in which "the only source of information about [social problems] and how to solve [them] comes from the agencies and corporations that benefit from exaggerating and distorting the information" (Baer and Chambliss, 1997: 88).

Sociologist Mark Fishman (1980) notes that there are consequences to assailing audiences with "agency accounts" of social life that "pass on to the public bureaucratic views of the world as plain fact" (1980: 136). Namely, politicians and corporate leaders who have the authority to relay their perspectives to us via popular culture and mass media can use that access to spread claims that are consistent with their own political or economic agenda, regardless of whether the claims are accurate or data-driven. For instance, public officials routinely disseminate authoritative claims about out-of-control crime problems that can only be combated with "get tough" approaches to law enforcement that require "waging war" on some illicit scourge like drugs or terrorism. Even though there is scant evident to suggest that hyper-punitive social control responses make society safer, these sorts of bold responses to social problems inevitably attract the attention of news agencies, resonate positively with citizens, and help them win reelection.

Although we live in a society that adheres to the ideals of freedom of speech and thought, claims-makers are always directing toward us messages about why we should espouse *their values* and the benefits of compliance to the prevailing social order. In fact, from a young age we are socialized to believe the choices we make and ideas we believe are all our own, and that we choose all on our own to follow or disregard the rules of society. Yet, our individual and collective thoughts about the social problems affecting our lives are inevitably influenced by the messages about authority, respect, and loyalty that we consume through popular culture.

KEY QUESTIONS

What is the difference between insider and outsider claims-makers? Why are insiders better positioned to use popular culture as a vehicle to spread their claims?

Popular entertainment is often used to disseminate propaganda and reinforce established institutional views of social issues to a mass audience. What examples of propaganda can you identify in popular entertainment?

In the aftermath of mass emergencies and public tragedies, public officials often use popular culture to spread their claims about the reasons for the tragic events or to advance their preferred response to the problem. Why is this the case and what makes popular culture such a valuable tool for this purpose? Can you identify examples of this use of popular culture in the wake of a recent high-profile tragedy?

SUGGESTED READINGS

Altheide, D.L. (2013) "Media logic, social control, and fear", *Communication Theory*, 23(3): 223-38.

Fishman, M. (1980) *Manufacturing the news*, Austin, TX: University of Texas Press.

Tepper, S.J. (2009) "Stop the beat: Quiet regulation and cultural conflict", *Sociological Forum*, 24(2): 276-306.

FIVE

Popular Culture and Pushback

"If I may, I would like to dedicate my performance and this
award to the transgender community. Thank you, thank you,
thank you, for your courage, for your inspiration, thank you
for your patience, and thank you for letting us be part of the
change."

These were the remarks of Jeffrey Tambor, delivered on-stage at the 2015
Golden Globes Awards as he accepted the "Best Actor" award for his
portrayal of Maura Pfefferman, a transgender character on the critically
acclaimed television series, *Transparent*. The series, which premiered late
in 2014, chronicles the fictional Maura's gender transition along with
the experiences of family and friends as they try to incorporate this
transition into their own complicated lives. Since its debut, *Transparent*
has drawn nearly universal praise from television critics and won or
been nominated for numerous awards. For many activists this sort of
adulation – in the form of ratings, awards, and the renewal of the show
itself for future seasons – hints at a cultural shift regarding traditional
definitions of gender and various heteronormative social mores. From this
perspective, popular culture products like *Transparent* are more than just
entertainment; they are important drivers of social change. This notion is
evident in Tambor's comments, particularly his closing remarks: "Thank
you for letting us be part of the change." But what is Tambor really saying
in invoking "change" in this way? If we return to a fundamental point
made throughout this book – that what we think of as social problems
are the result of claims-makers successfully defining an issue in a certain
way – then we can see that the "change" being discussed here reflects
the idea that traditional notions of gender and appropriate sexuality are
being redefined, and popular culture is an important force in that shift.

A seemingly infinite number of social concerns swirl around us every day. Some of these become full-blown social problems that lots of people worry about, or politicians pledge to combat, or policymakers attempt to deal with. Many of these concerns do not come to be seen as social problems. This is because an issue of social concern must be transformed into a social problem, and this is a matter of effectively defining the issue as troublesome and in need of remedy. Successful definitions, however, do not simply emerge out of thin air; they are a product of the efforts of committed claims-makers and activists, many of whom actively seek to influence how people see the world around them, which is precisely why popular culture can be a significant part of how definitions of social problems get created and communicated. This chapter explores a different dynamic by focusing on how popular culture can be used to contest widely held beliefs associated with a particular social issue and promote or reflect social change in society at large. Compared to what has been discussed in previous chapters, these popular cultural forms are distinctive in the messages they communicate about social problems because they are created and shared with the express purpose of altering *established* definitions of a social issue. For instance, musicians sometimes challenge the status quo through protest songs, like Bob Dylan's "Masters of War" and Esperanza Spalding's "We are America," which calls for the closing of the Guantanamo Bay detention center; or when artists use graffiti and murals as displays of social commentary; or even when a comedian uses humor as a mechanism for challenging political authority. Popular television shows like *South Park* and *Family Guy* also use popular culture as a means to satirically make fun of or question established ways of seeing social issues.

Pushback

The idea that popular culture can serve as a means of pushback to debunk dominant meanings or established viewpoints, and promote alternative understandings of social issues, encourages us to more broadly consider the role of popular culture in the social problems process. Through pushback, popular culture can spur audiences to see existing issues from new perspectives, which in turn can reinvigorate definitional battles and create opportunities to introduce revised or oppositional claims. Since there are rarely instances when everyone agrees about what is or is not a social problem, claims-makers' attempts to depict conditions as harmful and in need of redress often generate counterclaims that challenge the original claims and perhaps frame the issues differently. Some will fashion their claims around the commonly accepted view of a social problem – as was evident in the previous chapters on *blaming* and *spreading* – while others will attempt to dispute and delegitimize those widely held beliefs in an effort to promote alternative views of that problem.

As this chapter will detail, pushback occurs when claimants use popular culture to challenge the status quo and reframe popular perceptions of social problems. The idea that popular culture can facilitate alternative ways of understanding social issues is an extension of the concept of *détournement* (see Debord and Wolman, 1956), which occurs when the various forms, products, and artifacts consumed via mass media and popular culture are reappropriated with radical and subversive meanings. The aim is to make people uncomfortable by strategically disrupting the cultural symbols they associate with the proper functioning of the social order, to reveal the hidden ideological propaganda being conveyed through them to the public. Recognizable examples of *détournement* include the cynical reframing of art, music, and other cultural forms in an attempt to expose abuses of corporate or political power.

Much like *détournement*, pushback sometimes occurs when claims-makers deliberately repurpose elements of popular culture in order to fashion claims that overtly challenge commonly held assumptions about social problems. The street artist Banksy has gained considerable notoriety in recent years for using graffiti as a medium for political activism. Other examples of this sort of pushback can include defacing a work of art or corporate logos in an attempt to alter their meaning. For instance, in 2013, the animal rights activist group People for the Ethical Treatment of Animals (PETA) sought to raise public awareness of medical experiments conducted on lab animals that are funded by the NFL, in hopes of developing new treatments for sports-related injuries (see Glasspiegel, 2013). As part of their campaign, PETA modified the NFL's shield to include dripping blood and an abused lab rat in place of a football, along with the tagline "unnecessary roughness." In a similar response to the revelation that steroid and performance enhancing drug (PED) usage is rampant in Major League Baseball (MLB), there emerged cynical representations of the MLB logo featuring a needle-injecting ballplayer. In these instances, claimants were attempting to reshape or modify the respective public images of these corporations (ie the NFL and MLB) as entities that condone problematic behavior, like the abusive

An example of *détournement*

Image creator: Joe Wolf : https://archive.org/details/flickr-ows-AbbeyRoadPepperSpray
ed-6385281835

treatment of animals and cheating players who enhance performance using illegal substances.

It is important to recognize, however, that pushback can also occur in more subtle ways, like when claims are assimilated into everyday forms of popular culture (eg sporting events, television programming, or motion pictures). Pushback, then, can be found both embedded in everyday popular culture – as reflected in shows like *Transparent* and *Looking*, representing the experiences of LGBTQ populations – and through efforts to defiantly reappropriate popular culture by artists like Pussy Riot, the Russian feminist punk rock protest group, whose members were arrested and imprisoned for hooliganism following a guerrilla performance inside a Moscow cathedral in 2012. Regardless of whether it occurs through overt, in-your-face means, or in a subtler fashion, pushback can help to reinvigorate the definitional battles that are ongoing in the life cycle of a social problem; this in turn creates opportunities for alternative views and definitions to gain traction.

To clarify this point, think about the work of photographers who attempt to document the atrocities of war through images of war-strewn villages, the bodies of soldiers killed during combat, and the flag-draped caskets of slain troops. As artistic forms, the visual imagery of still photography and moving pictures can have a jarring effect on individual and public perceptions by exposing the most intimately horrifying and violent aspects of war, which are impossible to comprehend by civilians who do not fight in wars and are regularly audience to the claims made by politicians that emphasize the virtue of combat. When policymakers seeking public support for the military actions they authorize, sanitize the realities of war, violent death is often framed as glorious sacrifice, and acts of imperialism as spreading democracy to people victimized by oppression. Political leaders have historically presented military aggression as an unfortunate but unavoidable part of modern life, often portraying it as the only viable means of protecting national interests. With this definition of war rigidly in place, audience members are expected to accept these claims as their patriotic duty and to follow along in "supporting the war" through military service, volunteerism, or even just by not criticizing leaders and their actions.

War, of course, is sometimes necessary, but the larger point is that bureaucrats have sufficient power in the public sphere to frame popular discourse about the value and inviolable necessity of military combat. Photographic and video imagery, however, can expose otherwise hidden elements of social problems in ways that challenge, contradict, and otherwise refute the claims being made by political leaders and other institutional actors (see Meyrowitz, 1994; Doyle, 2003). For example, during the 1960s, television news footage played an important role in shifting social attitudes about civil rights and American war efforts, because people could now view from their own homes nightly news footage of protesters being beaten by police, and of American soldiers lying dead and wounded on the combat fields of Vietnam. Consequently, a growing number of people began to press policymakers to enact civil rights reform and popular sentiment eventually turned against the Vietnam War. Regardless of whether or not it was the intent of those news agencies, photographers, and journalists to challenge dominant social definitions of racial inequality and the necessity of war, the images themselves nonetheless constituted pushback because they generated alternative framings that facilitated (or, perhaps, fortified) shifting public perceptions in favor of racial equality and in opposition to the Vietnam War. Keep in mind, none of this occurred in absolutes – there were still plenty of segregationists and war supporters in the US during the 1960s. Yet public sentiment on aggregate was shifting, and pushback through popular culture played an important role in that process.

Packaging counterclaims in popular culture: *Pit Bulls and Parolees*

Pushback can be found in all sorts of styles and popular culture. For instance, pushback can be located in the reality television show *Pit Bulls and Parolees*. Now, it may seem odd to conceptualize pushback by focusing on problems – the dangers of pit bulls and difficulties faced by parolees trying to reintegrate into society – that most people might not think about all that much, and a show that airs on a niche cable network like Animal Planet. But it offers an illustrative example of pushback because the show has been expressly created to use popular culture as a way of reframing commonly held assumptions that pit bulls and parolees have little value because they are inherently dangerous to the public.

Pit bulls and parolees alike have long been subject to stereotypes and widespread negative portrayals. Inmates, for example, anticipate being stigmatized by the public after being released from incarceration, which may negatively affect their ability to obtain (and maintain) meaningful employment and lead them to "accept stereotypes as being true of the self and feel devalued as a result" (Moore et al, 2013: 527). These fears are not without reason. Ex-convicts face considerable social bias and in many areas have basic rights, such as the ability to vote, blocked or severely restricted. Furthermore, most communities are not prepared to provide adequate support for released prisoners attempting to reintegrate into society, which increases the likelihood that these individuals will respond violently, end up homeless, and eventually return to jail or prison (see Petersilia, 2000). Pit bulls are similarly framed in popular culture and media reports as mean, hyper-aggressive animals that pose a grave threat to society, particularly children. A recent poll of Americans offers insights into just how entrenched these views are. Fully half of those polled reported they would not consider a pit bull when adopting a dog. In fact, many would not be comfortable living in the same residential neighborhood as pit bulls (40%), while overall 59% consider the breed to be somewhat dangerous (35%) or very dangerous (24%) (Swanson, 2014). A 2014 *Time* article, titled "The trouble with pit bulls," encapsulates the sorts of claims that have fueled these widespread public perceptions of pit bulls. The article begins with a profile of a three-year-old girl whose face was mauled when three pit bulls "broke down the door to [her] grandfather's house and mauled the toddler until half her face was paralyzed and she lost the use of one of her eyes." The piece, which includes a picture of the young child's disfigured face, attempts to bolster its claim with a bevy of facts and figures, noting that: "Pit bulls make up only 6% of the dog population, but they're responsible for 68% of dog attacks and 52% of dog-related deaths since 1982" (Alter, 2014). *Pit Bulls and Parolees* uses the conventions of reality television programming to fashion and present counterclaims to the dominant social definitions of pit bulls and ex-convicts. The show, which first aired in 2009, depicts the day-to-day operations of the Villalobos Rescue Center. Tia Torres, the shelter's founder, says that both the shelter and the show share the goal of proving to the public when "the 'bad boys' of society meet the so-called 'bad boys' of the canine community ... they bring out a side of each other that's sweet, warm and unbelievably touching" (see www. animalplanet.com/tv-shows/pitbulls-and-parolees/about-this-show/ about-pit-bulls-and-parolees/). As the title suggests, this show is about more than just one problematized category. In addition to rescuing and retraining pit bulls, the shelter owner pairs them with ex-convicts, many of whom must wrestle with a perception problem similar to what pit bulls face (ie they are often seen as inherently deviant and utterly incapable of reformation). Thus, the show's creators are trying to counter entrenched definitions that mark pit bulls *and* ex-convicts as extremely dangerous to society and replace them with definitions that celebrate the many virtues of pit bulls (inherently loving and obedient) and former offenders (caring and compassionate individuals who are more than just a reflection of their past actions). In other words, this show – which at first glance looks like just one of the many reality programs one might find while browsing television channels – has been intentionally designed to directly challenge the fixed understandings of these categories and replace them with less stigmatizing social definitions.

The claims being relayed to audiences in *Pit Bulls and Parolees* reflect just one example of pushback, which can also be found in all manners of popular culture, including movies, music, fashion, and even the sardonic social commentary of comics like Louis C.K., George Carlin, and Chris Rock. Each of these examples reinforces a fundamental underlying idea of pushback: that the processes and products of popular culture can be – and routinely are – repurposed as vehicles for social problems claims-making. To better understand this point, it is useful to think about how social problems are both generated and combatted through recognizable popular culture forms like professional sports, music, and television.

Box 5.1: Archie Bunker and pushback

During the 1970s, television audiences bore witness to stark portrayals of bigotry that helped define how popular culture can be used to push back against social problems. None of this was without controversy, as a disclaimer that aired before the 1971 premier episode of *All in the Family* suggests: "The program you are about to see is *All in the Family*. It seeks to throw a humorous spotlight on our frailties, prejudices and concerns. By making them a source of laughter, we hope to show—in a mature fashion—just how absurd they are" (Nussbaum, 2014). Centered on the lives of a cantankerous bigot named Archie Bunker, and his family and friends, *All in the Family* used crass language (such as open usage of the n-word) and discrimination to address issues like racism, sexism, homophobia, anti-Semitism, abortion, rape, and other topics previously deemed too controversial for a comedy program.

> A Republican loading-dock worker living in Queens, Bunker railed from his easy chair against "coons" and "hebes," "spics" and "fags." He yelled at his wife and he screamed at his son-in-law, and even when he was quiet he was fuming about "the good old days." (Nussbaum, 2014)

Throughout much of the series, Bunker was constantly surrounded by evidence of the social progress he found so difficult to accept. His son-in-law, Mike, is a *pinko* socialist who is regularly insulted for having no common sense; his daughter, Gloria, an independent young woman and unabashed feminist;

his best friend, "Stretch" Cunningham, was Jewish (a fact unbeknownst to Archie until Cunningham's death); and neighbor George Jefferson, an affluent African American who believes God is black and shares similar bigoted tendencies, often calling white people *honkies*, *crackers*, and *zebras* if their parents were multi-racial. And, of course, his wife Edith, who most of the time acted as a second-class citizen in her own home, until it was time to speak up and show Archie the error of his ways.

Still, Archie Bunker has a lovable quality because he is ignorant of his own bigotry, and in trying to do the right thing exposes the foolishness of intolerance. He admires his friend George Jefferson because he is "one of the good ones," which to Archie is a hard-working and law-abiding black man; and when confronted with overt hatred, like when the KKK intends to burn a cross, Archie expresses repulsion and proclaims he and his "black blood brothers" are going to "bust [their] honky heinies." Likewise, in a 1971 episode, Bunker famously learns that one of his buddies – a former American football player – was gay. Bunker naturally associated homosexuality with effeminate male *fairies*, noting that, "A guy who wears glasses is a four-eyes. A guy who's a fag is a queer." Yet, Bunker was forced to confront his own intolerance upon realizing that Steve, a masculine, well-kept, single man who shares many of Bunker's conservative political beliefs, could be gay despite not physically coinciding with his mental image of how a gay man should look and act.

At the time, CBS expected these sorts of depictions to be rebuked by offended viewers (see Nussbaum, 2014), but *All in the Family* went on to become the most popular show on television and inspired similar socially conscious primetime sitcoms like *The Jeffersons*, *Maude*, *Good Times*, and *Soap*. On one hand, the success of these shows indicates how television and popular culture can be a force for pushback that prompts audiences to reject hatred and promote equality. On the other, many viewers flocked to characters like Bunker not because they disavowed what he stood for, but rather because his common man bigotry allowed fans to see "him as one of their own" (Nussbaum, 2014, see also Austerlitz, 2014).

Pushback and professional sports

In February of 2014, Michael Sam was a star college football player preparing to enter the NFL draft when he announced publicly that he is homosexual. Occurring not long after both Major League Soccer (MLS) player Robbie Rogers and Jason Collins, a professional basketball player in the NBA, made their own pronouncements in 2013, Sam's disclosure was significant to many observers because he was expected to be the first openly gay player drafted into the National Football League (NFL). Of course, by this time numerous female athletes had already disclosed their sexual orientation, including Billie Jean King, Martina Navratilova, Britney Griner, and Megan Rapinoe; and Justin Fashanu had long since become the first openly gay male footballer to compete in Britain while a member of Leeds United in 1990. Yet Sam's admission was nonetheless viewed as a monumental moment in the larger fight for equal rights. In an article published by *Fox Sports*, for example, former NFL linebacker Brendon Ayanbadejo touted Sam's announcement as the start of a "ground-breaking voyage that in many ways is similar to those of Jackie Robinson and Rosa Parks – extraordinary moments in the push for equality" (Ayanbadejo, 2014). It might seem like hyperbole to compare Sam's announcement to the civil rights achievements of Robinson (who broke baseball's color barrier in 1947) and Parks (whose refusal to give up her seat on a public bus to a white passenger in 1955 was a momentous act of social disobedience in direct defiance of Jim Crow segregation). But Sam's actions also affected longstanding social norms and institutional policies barriers that have devalued, discriminated against, and otherwise harmed people of varying non-heterosexual orientations. The days after Sam's announcement were filled with proclamations from distinguished journalists, television personalities, fellow athletes, social media users and politicians. For instance, in *Sports Illustrated*, Sam's announcement was called "one of those seminal moments" in which we see how "the events that truly transcend sports are the ones that change the face of our culture" (Mandel, 2014). Although many athletes and pundits were openly critical of Sam and suggested he would have a detrimental impact on the sports world, Sam's announcement and the public responses it generated – both favorable and unfavorable – nonetheless highlight how popular culture facilitated the fashioning and dissemination of claims that challenged conventional definitions of "appropriate sexuality" in and out of sports.

We can also see how sports offer avenues for pushback related to other social issues. One of the more famous historical examples occurred during the 1936 Summer Olympics in Berlin, Germany, when Jackie Owens single-handedly quashed the Nazi myth of Aryan superiority simply by participating and winning four gold medals in front of Adolf Hitler. Likewise, during the 1968 Summer Olympics, American athletes Tommie Smith and John Carlos infused protest within their athletic competition when they famously bowed their heads and raised black-gloved fists during their medal ceremony to protest ongoing political, social, and economic maltreatment of African Americans and other oppressed people. Both Smith and Carlos were so vilified for their audacious act of defiance that they would later receive death threats. Interestingly, Australian sprinter Peter Norman, who shared the podium with Smith and Carlos, wore a human rights pin in solidarity with their protest, and was similarly ostracized for his actions (see Frost, 2008).

More recently, the integration of professional sports with the social problems process was on display when, in December 2014, LeBron James and other high-profile basketball players wore shirts emblazoned with the slogan "I can't breathe" on the court prior to their scheduled game. The phrase held special significance because they were the words that Eric Garner had repeated more than 10 times, on July 17, 2014, as he died while a New York City police officer held him in a chokehold (the officer was attempting to apprehend Garner for selling individual cigarettes, known as "loosies"). The phrase became a slogan among protestors following a jury's decision not to indict the officer. It also became part of the larger Black Lives Matter movement that had emerged in response to the controversial 2014 police shooting of Michael Brown in Ferguson, Missouri and the alarming prevalence of unarmed African-American men and boys being killed under questionable circumstances by police officers in the United States.

Pushback and the evolution of homosexuality in primetime television

One area where entertainment media have evolved over the years is the portrayal of LGBTQ characters in television. Historically, gay characters were rarely featured in primetime television (Gross and Woods, 1999), and when they were it was typically as a target for derisive social commentary or a source of comedic relief. For decades, any representation of gay characters on television and in film tended to paint a caricaturized portrait and perpetuate negative stereotypes of LGBTQ people (Russo, 1987; Gross and Woods, 1999). As Raley and Lucas (2006) note: "Gay males, Lesbians, and Bisexuals have been stereotypically portrayed as funny clowns, flaming queers, queens, fairies, fags, and flits; villainous criminals, mental patients, child molesters, and vampires; or victims of violence, HIV/AIDS, and gender/sexual identity disorder" (1987: 23). Critical observers have argued that these representations did not simply materialize during the late 20th century as an outgrowth of LGBTQ Americans becoming more culturally visible – many were compelled to present themselves publicly as heterosexual – but rather because "pressure by gay liberation directed the course that television would take regarding the presentation of homosexuality for the American viewer, and it succeeded in obtaining a more balanced and certainly a more prolific dialogue on television" (Russo, 1987: 221).

By the 1990s, however, it was possible to find incremental changes in how LGBTQ characters were being presented to television audiences. In 1997, for instance, Ellen DeGeneres's character boldly declared, "I'm gay" on her primetime sitcom, *Ellen*. A year later *Will & Grace*, which featured several prominent gay characters, premiered on NBC, where it was among the most popular shows on television during many of its nine seasons. A recent report from the British Broadcasting Corporation detailing "how TV advanced gay rights" (BBC, 2014) lauded these and other programs (such as *Six Feet Under, Glee, Orange is the New Black*, and *Modern Family*) for reshaping popular perceptions of gay persons, same-sex marriage, and a host of related issues that have traditionally been considered social problems.

In 2012, Vice President Joe Biden appeared on *Meet the Press* and stated in no uncertain terms that television played a transformative role in changing public views of homosexuality: "I think '*Will & Grace*' probably did more to educate the American public than almost anybody's done so far. People fear that which is different. Now they're beginning to understand" (NBC News, 2012). Biden is essentially arguing that popular culture helped to challenge – or pushback – against the longstanding narrow constructions of what it means to be homosexual in modern society and, in so doing, opened audiences to new ways of seeing, and created opportunities for new definitions to emerge.

There is evidence to suggest that change is occurring, though it continues to be much slower than many issue advocates would like to see. Each year GLAAD (formerly the Gay & Lesbian Alliance Against

Defamation) produces a "Where we are on TV" report, which tracks the representation of LGBT characters on scripted primetime television. A review of the 2015–16 television season found that 4% of regular characters (35 of 881) were identified as gay, lesbian, or bisexual (GLAAD, 2015). This is down slightly from the high-water mark of 4.4% noted in the organization's 2012–13 report but still well above the 1.1% found in its review of programming during the 2007–08 season. These data are important because they reflect how popular culture – in this case television programming – can be used to facilitate pushback and promote a changing set of meanings for various social issues. At the same time, the data also remind us that such depictions cannot necessarily cure social problems. In the United States, the majority of Americans now support same-sex marriage and almost 70% believe "gay or lesbian relations between consenting adults" should be legal – up from 32% in 1986 (Gallup, 2016). Of course, this means about 30% of the population still believe that LGBTQ people should be prosecuted as criminals for engaging in non-heterosexual relations, and there remain widespread instances of homophobic discrimination in the US and across the world. In fact, while nearly 20 nations recognize same-sex marriage and grant basic human rights to LGBTQ citizens, about 70 other countries maintain laws criminalizing homosexuality with severe punishments that can include life in prison or even death.

In most westernized nations, LGBTQ citizens might not need to worry about being imprisoned or executed for their sexual orientation, but they continue to be discriminated against in a variety of ways – some of which are reflected in popular culture. Back in 1997, Ellen DeGeneres's now famous "I'm gay!" admission was considered so controversial it compelled the ABC network to begin subsequent episodes with a parental advisory message. Two decades later it might seem inconceivable that audiences had to be warned a show might contain a gay character. But in truth it was not that long ago when merely the suspected presence of an LGBTQ cast member could halt the entire production of a film or television show. At the height of the HIV/AIDS epidemic during the 1980s, many celebrities refused to work alongside known or suspected homosexual actors (see Benshoff and Griffin, 2006). Furthermore, LGBTQ characters and gay-themed storylines were often little more than plot devices to lampoon *fags* and *queers* (eg the comedic farce of Tom Hanks and Peter Scolari in drag on *Bosom Buddies*), play upon persistent social fears of homosexuality and its effect on heterosexual family members (eg the villainous and psychotic gay characters in movies like *Cruising*); portray the turmoil triggered by someone being gay (eg *Boys Don't Cry*), or depict homosexuality as a phase in the adolescent rite of passage to becoming a heterosexual adult (eg the passionate yet fleeting lesbian tryst in *Personal Best*) (see Russo, 1987).

Notwithstanding the growing prevalence of homosexuality in primetime television and film, there is plenty of evidence to suggest these same stereotypes remain persistent in popular entertainment. Films such as *The Birdcage* and television shows like *Will & Grace* conspicuously contrast a logically thinking gay character who could pass as straight, with a comically emotional, unstable, and flamboyantly effeminate companion. Similarly, the character Lloyd Lee (played by Rex Lee) on *Entourage* was regularly presented in ways that positioned his homosexuality as a contradiction of the show's idealized vision of the unbridled machismo and rampant heterosexuality that characterize Hollywood; and this was exemplified by the persistent demeaning ethnic and homophobic ridicule from his boss Ari Gold. So while it might seem commonplace and somewhat normal these days to see LGBTQ characters in popular films and television programs, their representations continue to reflect the profound heteronormativity of mainstream popular culture and ongoing attempts to pushback against the discrimination and marginalization of LGBTQ people that still exist.

The popular sitcom *Modern Family* is a good example of the varied forms that pushback can take. In particular, it reminds us that pushback need not be abrasive or overt, or even look like there is much "pushing" going on. With *Modern Family*, most of the show's episodes since its debut in 2009 do not directly tackle topics related to same-sex marriage or homosexuality. Instead, the very structure of this show – which features an ensemble of related families and their friends – simply normalizes gay marriage by including a same-sex couple (the characters Cam and Mitch) and their adopted daughter within its storylines. Though Cam and Mitch's sexual orientation is sometimes used for comedic effect, it is primarily presented as just a normal part of the social world within which these characters exist.

As depictions of LGBTQ characters increase – albeit minimally, given GLAAD's finding that just 4% of regular characters were identified as gay, lesbian, or bisexual – there is also evidence to suggest that public perceptions of these issues are changing. A study on religion and public life conducted by the Pew Research Center found that a majority of Americans (55%) polled in 2015, support same-sex marriage, a rate driven in large part by strong support among millennials (70%) and respondents representing generation X (59%) (Pew Research Center, 2015); and 27% of respondents in a 2012 *Hollywood Reporter* poll of likely voters said that the representation of gay characters on TV increased their pro-marriage beliefs (Appelo, 2012). *The Atlantic* referred to this as "the Modern Family effect," arguing that "film and TV have helped popularize the idea that gay couples can be 'normal' – as banal as Cam and Mitch; as in dire need of counseling as Cyrus and James on *Scandal*; as loving parental as Stef and Lena on *The Fosters*" (Kornhaber, 2015). Given the modest increase in these representations since the turn of the century, as well as the shifting attitudes during that same time frame, there is indeed reason to suggest that popular culture has played a role in both perpetuating homophobic stereotypes and challenging long-dominant heteronormative ideologies by offering more tolerant and progressive definitions for public consideration.

The "It Gets Better" campaign

One of the more vivid examples of pushback against LGBTQ discrimination is the "It Gets Better Project" (IGBP), which was created in September 2010 by Dan Savage – a media personality and activist well known for his syndicated sex advice column and podcast – in response to the suicide deaths of several teens who had faced considerable harassment and bullying largely due to their sexual identities. Savage's celebrity as a kind of spokesperson for issues related to teen sexuality made him a much sought after voice for those seeking to make sense of these issues. On its website, IGBP describes its mission as: "to communicate to lesbian, gay, bisexual and transgender youth around the world that it gets better, and to create and inspire the changes needed to make it happen." This statement reflects their aim to "pushback" against prevailing heteronormative standards and other structures that provide cultural support for interpersonal aggression, such as bullying and other forms of harassment.

By many metrics IGBP has been successful since it was first introduced, generating more than 50,000 user-created videos that have been viewed more than 50 million times.

> To date, the project has received submissions from celebrities, organizations, activists, politicians and media personalities,

including President Barack Obama, Secretary of State
Hillary Clinton, Rep. Nancy Pelosi, Adam Lambert, Anne
Hathaway, Colin Farrell, Matthew Morrison of *Glee*, Joe
Jonas, Joel Madden, Ke$ha, Sarah Silverman, Tim Gunn,
Ellen DeGeneres, Suze Orman, the staffs of The Gap, Google,
Facebook, Pixar, the Broadway community, and many more.
For us, every video changes a life. It doesn't matter who makes
it. (www.itgetsbetter.org/pages/about-it-gets-better-project/)

With a message that resonates strongly with everyday citizens and
impressive celebrity endorsements, the IGBP has rapidly emerged as "a
worldwide movement" in the struggle to end LGBTQ discrimination and
"inspire hope for young people facing harassment" (see www.itgetsbetter.
org/pages/about-it-gets-better-project/). Savage and his colleague Terry
Miller have even curated the video submissions and selected about 100 of
them to be included in the book *It Gets Better: Coming Out, Overcoming
Bullying, and Creating a Life Worth Living* (2011), which appeared on *The
New York Times* bestseller list.

From a social problems perspective, IGBP offers an interesting case
study because it was conceptualized to be a movement fueled almost
entirely by elements of popular culture (eg YouTube and other social
media, as well as recruiting celebrities to echo and extend its messages).
IGBP's immersion in popular culture has enabled its contributors to
fashion deeply personal and relatable claims that seem like conversations
from caring adults (who have *been there*) to youth facing challenges.
Moreover, the Project's reliance on social media provides "a channel
through which LGBT adults could circumvent social and institutional
barriers to communication" (Jones, 2015: 319), and this arguably allows
those advocating IGBP's claims to be somewhat less reliant on the
traditional gatekeeping elements of problem discovery and construction
– namely, the need to first obtain mainstream media attention to spread
the message in order to rally public support and inspire political action
(although it should be noted that it was news coverage of LGBTQ teen
suicides that prompted Savage to start IGBP).

Some, however, have argued that for all its seeming successes, the
It Gets Better Project has not been as profound an agent of change as
many assume. For instance, Rattan and Ambady (2014) used the It Gets
Better Project as a case study to examine how people use and receive
social change messages. Using a sample of IGBP videos, they assessed
how target audiences processed and acted upon the information they

received. What they found was that IGBP messages tended to exhibit one of two features: (1) social connection (ie the idea that social support exists) and (2) social change (ie that steps are being taken to reduce prejudice). Interestingly, they noted that the vast majority of messages focused on aspects of social support, which led them to conclude that there was not much change actually being encouraged during the videos. The authors concluded that the prevalence of social connection messaging in IGBP videos is "less comforting to those targeted by bias than supportive messages communicating social change content" (Rattan and Ambady, 2014: 9).

In another study that raised concerns about the overall impact of IGBP, Kellinger and Levine (2016) examined the top 21 videos posted on the IGBP website, as well as the comments attached to them by online viewers. Their analysis revealed "that the majority of [respondents] place the onus on the victim to 'stick it out' and wait until they are older for the bullying to stop" (2016: 85), which they find problematic because "this 'while you wait' message also relieves the responsibility of anti-gay bullies and the current adults who should be responsible for protecting gay you and changing the culture of schools" (2016: 89). Although we should refrain from drawing conclusions about the efficacy of IGBP based on what people post online, Kellinger and Levine nonetheless echo the concerns advanced by Rattan and Ambady regarding the dangers of focusing too much on social support to the exclusion of a more decisive push for cultural and institutional changes.

The concerns raised by researchers and other critics about the IGBP's vague or possibly contradictory messages reinforce an important point about pushback. Namely, that there is an important distinction between *challenging an existing claim* and *effectively replacing that existing claim* with an alternative perspective. Through the efforts of advocacy groups like IGBP and its allied supporters, we have witnessed considerable shifts in public acceptance of LGBTQ equality in many parts of the world. Despite this progress, however, we may never see an end to the problem of LGBTQ discrimination because there will likely always be people and groups, and perhaps even nations as a whole, that rebuke efforts to reframe the issue of sexual orientation as a natural part of human existence. In North Carolina, for instance, the state legislature passed a "bathroom bill" in early 2016 that "requires students in state schools to use the bathroom that corresponds with the gender recorded on their birth certificates"; and Georgia lawmakers recently considered legislation that will allow faith-based groups to deny service to LGBTQ people in order to protect their religious liberty. Yet these measures have also been met with stern criticism, which indicates that the efforts of groups like IGBP are slowly but surely changing how people view the treatment of LGBTQ people in the United States and other parts of the world.

> Some of the biggest corporate names in the state including PayPal, Bank of America and Dow Chemical denounced the new [North Carolina] law. The NBA said the law could cost Charlotte the right to host the 2017 NBA All-Star game. It's scheduled to be held at Time Warner Cable Arena, where the Charlotte Hornets play. In Georgia ... the measure has been met by outcries from major players in the business, tech and entertainment industries. The CEO of Salesforce said the company "can't have a program in Georgia" if [Governor Nathan Deal] signs it into law. Disney said it would stop filming in the state and Unilever said it would "reconsider investment" if it was signed. The NFL said the bill could cost Atlanta the opportunity to host the Super Bowl. Georgia Prospers, which represents over 480 companies, also denounced the bill. Several big companies are members of the group, including Coca-Cola, Delta, Home Depot, UPS and Marriott. (Garcia, 2016)

If these corporate responses tell us anything, it is that popular sentiment in the United States is now firmly against the overt discrimination of people based on their sexual orientation, and it undoubtedly played a role in prompting Georgia Governor Nathan Deal to veto that state's bill. Yet it is important to remember that we are only now starting to see a cultural shift away from the prevailing mentality that homosexuality is antithetical to American values, which historically prompted "oppressive assumptions" about LGBTQ people that reinforced "the closeted mentalities of gay people themselves" (Russo, 1987: xi). As a catalyst for progress and change, however, popular culture can stimulate people to question assumptions and beliefs, or just generate discussion about various social problems. Consequently, using popular culture to raise awareness and facilitate pushback can be a vital force in the social problems process because it can reinvigorate definitional battles and create pathways for new claims to enter the debate in hopes of gaining traction.

Box 5.2: The internet and WikiLeaks

The internet has become an indispensable vehicle of popular culture in modern society, as well as a burgeoning medium for disseminating social problem claims – including those that involve pushback. Perhaps no single entity reflects these trends more than the international non-profit WikiLeaks, which since 2006 has used the internet to publish millions of classified government documents and information received from anonymous sources around the world. Under the stewardship of the controversial and quasi-celebrity editor-in-chief Julian Assange, WikiLeaks combines traditional investigative journalism with the radicalism of high-tech hacktivism by using computer networks to expose corporate and governmental corruption. Amnesty International has praised these efforts, crediting WikiLeaks for fostering political transparency and fueling popular uprisings against oppressive regimes, including the 2010 Arab spring.

If public and media responses to WikiLeaks' disclosures are any indication, then the group has been wildly successful in exposing political inner circles and achieving social and political relevance. In many ways, WikiLeaks has rewritten the playbook on networked claims making in cyberspace, because it does not simply direct newsworthy claims toward journalists; it has made that information publicly available on a mass scale directly to the global citizenry. On the surface it seems that WikiLeaks has had a transcendent effect on public life. The idea that a relatively small bunch of activists could get access to and distribute so many sensitive materials in many ways spurred a new era of networked online political activism (see Maratea, 2014). But these successes did not come without cost as anger in political circles over the leaks generated a scathing institutional response. Military and public officials in the US have launched damaging counter-claims at WikiLeaks, proclaiming the group guilty of distributing anti-war propaganda and engaging in treasonous conduct. Senate Republican leader Mitch McConnell and Vice-President Joe Biden both labeled Julian Assange a "high-tech terrorist", who should be prosecuted for damaging America's relationship with its allies and placing the lives of diplomats and informants at risk (CBS News, 2010; MacAskill, 2010; Siddique and Weaver, 2010), while former Arkansas Governor Mike Huckabee went so far as to suggest that people involved with WikiLeaks should be found guilty of treason and executed (Siddique and Weaver, 2010). Over time, the damage inflicted by these sorts of institutional counter-claims did thwart the promising potential of WikiLeaks as a cyber-claims-making entity. Although WikiLeaks remains in operation, it has, at times, had to shut down its website due to funding shortfalls (Whalen and Crawford, 2010). If WikiLeaks tells us anything, it is that internet facilitates powerful new forms of pushback that are global in scope; yet without continued sympathetic media coverage and institutional sponsorship it is unclear whether the pushback efforts of claimants like WikiLeaks will have lasting social relevance in the mind of average citizens.

Conclusion

Back in 1965, civil rights protesters marching from Selma to Montgomery, Alabama were brutally beaten by law enforcement acting on the authority of segregationist Governor George Wallace. Georgia Congressman John Lewis recently posted on his Facebook account how he and the other marchers "gave a little blood on the Edmund Pettis Bridge to dramatize to the nation that people of color were denied the right to vote." They succeeded in part because television news outlets aired the horrific imagery of peaceful African-American activists being violently beaten by troopers, to audiences around the country; the stark acts of racism on display in these broadcasts helped fuel a public outcry that played a big role in compelling President Lyndon Johnson to move forward with the Civil Rights Act of 1964 and the Voting Rights Act of 1965. The effect was undeniable: television – and popular culture more generally – could produce meaningful social change because when audiences could see with their own eyes the reality of what was going on around them, it inevitably shaped public opinion (Meyrowitz, 1994; Doyle, 2003).

Yet for all the ways popular culture can facilitate pushback and reshape perceptions of social issues, we must recognize that altered definitions are not the same as curing a social problem. Congressman Lewis made this point in his Facebook post, noting that, "We must honor the sacrifices of all those who marched, sacrificed, bled, and died" in the struggle for civil rights because "today, thousands of Americans are still being denied the right to vote." No matter how successful claimants are in raising awareness for a problem and affecting change, they nonetheless face ongoing barriers to maintaining credibility and relevance. After all, you may recall that some people cited the election of Barack Obama as President in 2008, as evidence that the United States has become a colorblind society where racism no longer exists. Yet one need not look very hard to conclude racial and economic discrimination continuous to flourish in the United States, whether it be reflected in the poisonous contamination of water supplies among poor and minority households in Flint, Michigan, the disproportionate incarceration and execution rates of non-white offenders, the economic red-lining of urban neighborhoods, the harsh school disciplining of African-American children as compared to white youth (Lewin, 2012), or even the violent responses against minority voters at Donald Trump campaign rallies during the 2016 presidential election. The point is that acts of pushback inevitably generate counterclaims designed to delegitimize social problems by minimizing the severity and harm they pose to society.

Successful instances of pushback not only draw oppositional claims, they also are at risk of being assimilated into dominant mainstream commercial culture. The problem is that pushback efforts over time can become so widely accepted that they become the norm, thereby allowing corporate, political, and bureaucratic authorities and institutions to co-opt those messages within mainstream culture and transform them into consumable commodities in a way that strips them of their revolutionary intent and meanings. When this occurs, the capacity for pushback efforts to challenge established views and promote social change may get lost through commercialization and corporatization. This is precisely why a television show about a transgender man like *Transparent* can achieve mainstream popularity and songs by a punk rock group like The Clash are now heard in commercial jingles even though their music was long ago considered anti-authoritarian and addressed matters of liberation and political injustice.

Hip-hop and rap also offer instructive lessons about the risks of pushback becoming commercialized for mass consumption. Artists like Tupac, NWA, KRS-One, Public Enemy, Talib Kweli, Killer Mike, and others, have all used popular culture as a medium for telling disaffected black youth to "fight the power" or otherwise relay feelings of anger and frustration at continued subjugation by political, social, economic, cultural, and even religious institutions. Yet as rap music and hip-hop culture have been mainstreamed through corporate commercialization for affluent white audiences not similarly affected by social policies that continue to discriminate, segregate, and oppress, the messages of resistance at the core of hip-hop have been diluted. Whereas Ice Cube, as a member of NWA, once told listeners to "fuck tha police" in protest of police brutality, you are now more likely to see him as a corporate spokesperson for Coors Lite beer. In fact, hip-hop more generally is now commonly depicted for mainstream consumption in association with the extravagant lifestyles of Jay-Z, Beyoncé, Kanye West, and Nicki Minaj, or through stories of how someone like Snoop Dogg now organizes youth football leagues.

None of this is to say that artists like Jay-Z fail to take political stands, or are now unwilling to use their form of popular culture as a vehicle for resistance. The backlash against Beyoncé's performance of "Formation" during the Super Bowl halftime show in early 2016 exemplifies this point. Critics suggested that her dance routine, which supposedly paid homage to the Black Panther Party, and the music video for "Formation" were "endangering law enforcement" through politicized imagery that could incite violence against police: "The video opens with the singer standing atop a half-submerged New Orleans police cruiser, a recurring image throughout. Other related symbols periodically flash on screen: sirens; a jacket that says 'POLICE' on it; graffiti that reads 'stop shooting us'" (Chokshi, 2016b). In response, the National Sheriffs' Association Executive Director Jonathan Thompson proclaimed that Beyoncé was "inciting bad behavior," and former New York Mayor Rudy Giuliani claimed the performance was "a platform to attack police officers who are the people who protect her and protect us, and keep us alive" (Chokshi, 2016a; 2016b).

If we can learn anything from the critical response to Beyoncé's Super Bowl rendition of "Formation" it is the potential paradox of successfully employing popular culture as a means of creating and communicating pushback. On one hand, it is indeed our ability to recognize and act in opposition to social power that make symbolic and collective responses to cultural authority so important to understand in the context of social problems work. Yet on the other hand, we must remain cognizant of the fact that popular culture is inexorably tied to state and corporate power, and that many of the cause-marketing campaigns done in the name of charity are often more effective at providing entertaining imagery and increasing profit margins than combating social problems. When pushback efforts are commercialized through popular culture they become corporatized economic commodities, marketed first and foremost to affluent people with money to spend. Consequently, the legitimacy of pushback as a strategy to confront a whole host of social problems is often determined by whether corporate interests and middle-class audiences adapt them into the dominant mainstream culture that perpetuates those very problems. This is not to suggest that all forms of pushback are doomed to fail through commercial acquisition. Rather, the real challenge is discerning when the pushback against social problems made through popular culture actually serves the public good by mobilizing public attention and resources towards the organizations, claimants, researchers, and policymakers actively working to cure a social problem. At the end of the day, social progress is inevitable, and popular culture will continue to function as both a vehicle for resistance and a mechanism for reasserting the status quo.

KEY QUESTIONS

How are new technologies – such as the internet, social media, smart phone cameras, law enforcement dashboard cameras, and so on – changing how we understand and respond to social problems in modern life? In what ways do these technologies facilitate pushback? How might these technologies encourage also audiences to conform to established or institutional definitions of social problems?

Imagine you are an activist fighting a social problem like climate change or income inequality. What forms of popular culture might you use to stimulate others to join in pushing back against opponents' views of that problem?

Plan a day that you will keep a detail log of your observations as you go about your normal daily activities. Take note of any forms of popular culture pushback you observe or experience, and consider whether or not they are shaping your perceptions of particular social issues.

SUGGESTED READINGS

Crane, D. (2000) "Women's clothing behavior as nonverbal resistance: Symbolic boundaries, alternative dress, and public space", in *Fashion and its social agendas: Class, gender, and identity in clothing*, Chicago, IL: University of Chicago Press, pp 99-131.

Jenkins, H., Shresthova,S,, Gamber-Thompson, L., Kligler-Vilenchik, N. and Zimmerman, A. (2016) *By any media necessary: The new youth activism*, New York: New York University Press.

Lim, M. 2012. "Clicks, cabs, and coffee houses: Social media and oppositional movements in Egypt, 2004–2011", *Journal of Communication*, 62(3): 231-48.

SIX

Marketing Social Problems
Through Popular Culture

Back in the early 20th century, Bayer Pharmaceuticals marketed
heroin as "the cheapest specific for the relief of coughs," while
other narcotics like cocaine, opium, and methamphetamines
were widely used in hospitals for medicinal purposes on both adults and
children. Even more, salesmen used to peddle various tonics and serums
they claimed would cure all sorts of medical maladies. One such creation
was a hangover cure and mood stabilizer named Bib-Label Lithiated
Lemon-Lime Soda; another was first manufactured in 1885, and sold
as an energizing brain tonic by a pharmacist named Charles Alderton.
Today you know these products as 7-Up and Dr Pepper respectively,
and you are probably quite aware that they serve no medicinal purpose.
At the time, however, they were marketed to a willing and perhaps
naïve public, as solutions to a variety of social problems. By modern
standards it is comical to think that anyone would try to convince you
that soft drinks are a cure for illness, or that hospitals should be
medicating patients with cocaine or heroin. But these days people are
being sold wristbands, ribbons, clothing, hashtags, fried chicken
buckets, and a variety of other symbolic and material goods under
the guise that consumption of these products will help solve all sorts
of social ills.

Popular culture is fueled in large part by the twin forces of
consumerism and consumption, which are often associated with
accumulating material goods. But we also acquire other things from
our interactions with popular culture, such as knowledge, shared ideals
and beliefs, symbolic commodities, and even personal or collective
identities. Just as you might purchase a car, smart phone, or concert
tickets, throughout our lives we procure thoughts, perceptions, and

information about the social world. This is precisely why claims-makers try so hard to grab our attention and sell us on their solutions to social problems. Their efforts are not really all that different from retailers who make commercials advertising all the reasons why we should buy their products. The difference is that claimants are selling beliefs about social problems in hopes of convincing people to support their points of view. In this way, the claims that we receive during media reports, press conferences, discussions, and debates, are essentially advertisements for the social problems being sold to us, as well as the possible solutions to cure them. And much like when you are watching a late night infomercial, once armed with what you believe is all the information needed to make an informed decision, you must then decide whether to buy the product – or the social problem – or change the channel and pay attention to something else.

Convincing the public to stay tuned in and remain concerned about a prospective social problem requires activists, politicians, journalists, and other claimants to present themselves and their issues in ways that capture our attention and seem meaningful. To better understand how they succeed in achieving their goals, we organize this chapter around two interrelated concepts. The first is *commodification*, which focuses on how popular culture accommodates the development of material goods that claims-makers use to market their problems to mass audiences. We see commodification in action when people purchase and display message-carrying products like clothing, bumper stickers, tote bags, and other merchandise as a show of support for a particular group or issue (see Smith, 1988; Santino, 1992; Endersby and Towle, 1996; Lilley et al, 2010). The second key concept to be examined in this chapter is *symbolic communities*; this refers to how people use popular culture to convey a sense of mutual values and how such displays serve to unify otherwise disparate people around a shared belief or issue. The adoption of symbols and adornments signifying support for a cause is an important, if somewhat overlooked, driver of the social problems process. When taken together, commodification allows social problems to be advertised in material form through popular culture, which are then displayed publicly in symbolic shows of solidarity among the community of supporters. When considering these concepts it is important to remember that social problems must achieve and maintain a perception of legitimacy if they are to receive the public and institutional support needed to remain in the spotlight. Having millions of people purchase t-shirts, place bumper stickers on their vehicles, or wear a wristband suggests that there is collective support for the idea that the particular issue is worthy of our collective attention and a social response.

Box 6.1: Burger King and The Proud Whopper

Cause marketing efforts can be global, national, and even local. To coincide with San Francisco's 44th annual Pride Celebration and Parade in July 2014, Burger King unveiled "The Proud Whopper", served in a rainbow colored wrapper inscribed with the message, "We are all the same inside." The catch, though, was The Proud Whopper was only served at one location, on San Francisco's Market Street, and was part of the fast food chain's "localized efforts to put into motion actions that support its recently-tweaked slogan: 'Be Your Way'" (Horovitz, 2014).

> At $4.29 it costs the same as a conventional Whopper. And, indeed, customers ultimately discover the only difference is the rainbow wrap... One gay rights activist says BK is doing the right thing. "Whenever a company comes out in support of gay people, it makes a difference" says Jordan Bach, a consultant to corporations on gay rights issues and a GLAAD media partner. "But when it's done right—when it's done with a campaign that shows the company understands diversity and really believes in the profound acceptance of other people—that sort of marketing can change minds and hearts at the deepest level." (Horovitz, 2014)

As part of the promotion, the Market Street location also distributed rainbow colored Burger King crowns to parade participants and observers, and proceeds from all Proud Whopper sales were donated for college scholarships benefitting graduating LGBT high school students.

Yet critics at the time suggested that while Burger King was promoting The Proud Whopper in press releases and YouTube videos, the company "appears to lack any substantial commitment to LGBT equality," and might have simply been trying to drum up sales and positive public relations despite not offering notably "trans-inclusive health care benefits to its employees, and ... no upper-level LGBT corporate programming" (Self, 2014). Burger King also supported Pride parades in other major cities and claimed The Proud Whopper was an effort to brand a welcoming "message of equality, self-expression, authenticity and just being who you are" (Steinmetz, 2014). Their efforts ultimately generated a range of counterclaims that ranged from questioning the company's marketing intent to lure "LGBTs to spend money on a company that does not live up to its claims" (Self, 2014), to "pro-traditional family" advocacy groups like American Family Association condemning the promotion for "promoting homosexual behavior as healthy and something to have pride in" (Murashko, 2014).

Commodification: the business of selling social problems

Perhaps you have seen television commercials depicting tragic scenes of suffering people or animals, as a narrator speaks over emotional music to ask whether you care enough to donate a small amount of money – often described less than the daily price of a cup of coffee – to help those in need. These examples reflect how the most compelling claims we receive about social problems – or any other matter of public importance, for that matter – are rarely generic, antiseptic, or stale in tone and content. To the contrary, they are persuasively packaged attempts to sell social problems. One of the key ways to do this is by cultivating a sense of personal connectedness between the claimant and audience members. This is done because people who feel an emotional attachment to an issue are more likely to engage in supportive action, such as donating money, attending rallies or dousing themselves with ice water, and displaying products like bumper stickers or coffee mugs that signal sponsorship of a cause.

These commercials also reveal another important element of the connections between popular culture and social problems – there is often a material or symbolic cost to consuming knowledge about any given social problem. For this reason, most social problems are marketed to the public in a manner not entirely dissimilar to material goods like clothing, electronics, and automobiles; and like the CEO of a commercial business, the claims-makers supplying the resources need to see an appropriate return on investment to support their activism and allow it to continue going forward. To be effective, claimants must mobilize the symbolic and material resources needed to sustain operations while accruing sufficient public recognition and political clout to achieve their goals (see McCarthy and Zald, 1977).

One way this is accomplished is through the leadership of a charismatic spokesperson who can effectively sell a social problem to the public. If you have ever seen video footage of the 1963 March on Washington for Jobs and Freedom, when more than 20,000 men and women in person, and millions more on television, witnessed Dr. Martin Luther King, Jr. deliver his now famous "I Have a Dream" speech, then you probably recognize how powerful claims can be when they strike a chord with the mass populace. The images and words from that event echoed so strongly that public officials faced intense pressure to institute legislative reform, which not coincidentally would happen shortly after with the passage of the Civil Rights Act of 1964 and the Voting Rights Act of 1965. In many ways, it was the captivating and magnetic leadership of Dr. King that compelled sympathetic mainstream media narratives about civil rights and the need for equality, which helped legitimate the movement and peacefully unite civil rights supporters across racial, ethnic, and economic lines. Additionally, efforts to coax people into recognizing the existence of a social problem can be accomplished using a variety of techniques like cold calling, pamphlet distribution, holding public events, communicating online and via social media, and most importantly, attracting media attention to the issue.

Yet all of these efforts are likely to fail if claims-makers fail to convince news agencies to direct media attention toward their efforts. The press holds a prominent role in shaping what people pay attention to in everyday life. This is referred to as the *agenda-setting* capacity of mainstream media and basically means journalists determine what is newsworthy for the public. Likewise, the issues, events, and people that news workers ignore are unlikely to be perceived as important by the general public. This is important when it comes to social problems because it underscores how much power news agencies have in determining what problems enter the news cycle and how long they remain there. It is therefore useful for those attempting to sell a social problem to be as persuasive as possible. A compelling "hook" is helpful when selling a problem to the media and, in turn, public audiences; and this is often achieved through things like clever wording or hashtags, evocative imagery, and empathy-inducing examples, such as a malnourished child or chained dog shivering in the snow. Popular culture often provides the catalyst needed for claims-makers to provide just that kind of hook.

Marketing social problems to mobilize support

When social problem claims become associated with popular culture, the imagery and goods that are produced can help carry claims forward by diffusing the message to new audiences and signaling widespread support for the idea that the problem exists, is important, and must be being combatted. The success in recent years of the "ice bucket challenge" exemplifies this sort of pop culture-infused "hook" and how it can help to sell a social problem. Originally conceived by a Boston College student named Pete Frates, after learning of his own amyotrophic lateral sclerosis (ALS) diagnosis (better known as Lou Gehrig's disease), the ice bucket challenge involved people recording videos of freezing water being dumped on their heads and then sharing those videos via social media, all with the aim of raising both awareness and funds to combat ALS. The challenge soon went viral online and seemingly spread to all corners of the globe, prompting countless people – from everyday citizens to politicians and famous celebrities – to get involved in fighting a disease many probably knew very little about. The idea was simple: when challenged, a person must either elect to take the ice bucket challenge and douse themselves with frigid water or donate money to ALS research (they may, of course, donate regardless of whether they accept the challenge), and then spread the word by challenging others via social media to do the same.

If anything, the success of the ice bucket challenge in raising funding for ALS research – over $100 million during the summer of 2014, compared to just $2.8 million the same period in 2013 (see Gallo, 2014) – exemplifies how marketing a problem via popular culture can exponentially increase public awareness and sympathy to that issue. As noted repeatedly throughout this book, social problems are about meanings more than anything else. We interact and engage with social problems in a variety of ways, from reading news reports to viewing heart-wrenching pictures, hearing tales of tragedy and sorrow, listening to political speeches, participating in polls and surveys, publishing tweets, and the list goes on. But these formats are all, at their core, vehicles for organizing and communicating meanings that influence individual and collective understandings of social problems.

Taking the Ice Bucket Challenge

© John Noonan: https://commons.wikimedia.org/wiki/File:August_26,_2014_Club_Meeting_with_TC_West_Band_and_ALS_Ice_Bucket_Challenge_(15046778691).jpg

Box 6.2: Online petitions and cyber-claims-making

The internet has become one of the most effective ways for claims-makers to sell social problems to the general public because online technology allows activists to sidestep mainstream media gatekeeping and rapidly communicate unfiltered information in real time, directly to prospective audiences. This ability for anyone with the proper equipment, a high-speed internet connection, and sufficient free time to cheaply publish content void of any governmental or institutional editorial oversight means online networks can facilitate communication among people that may be demographically disparate in real-world settings but share similar ideological orientations. In doing so, the internet can help claimants forge and reinforce a collective identity and commonality of purpose by "uniting individuals with shared experiences and beliefs and strengthening ties among them" (Perez, 2013: 79-80).

Among the most significant outcomes is that people and groups with little social power are using the internet to mobilize people in response to a variety of social problems and other causes. In 2012, for example, 13-year-old McKenna Pope started a petition on the cyber-activism website Change.org to urge the toy maker Hasbro to manufacture its Easy-Bake Oven in gender-neutral colors that would also appeal to boys. More than 44,000 signatures later, Pope and her family delivered the signatures to Hasbro's corporate headquarters, and the company responded by introducing new colors like black and silver to the product line (Grinberg, 2012). Of course, Hasbro had practical reasons for recognizing Pope and offering a supportive response. It provided an opportunity for good public relations, and expanding the available choices on a popular product would presumably be a catalyst for additional sales. Still, it no doubt speaks to the dynamism of internet technology when a young girl can initiate an otherwise innocuous appeal that garners so much public attention it compels a corporate reaction (see Maratea, 2014).

McKenna Pope's feel-good story notwithstanding, millions of online petitions and claims go virtually unnoticed every day, in part because most claimants still rely on journalists to draw attention to their efforts. In Pope's case, the press picked up on the compelling human-interest story of a girl taking on a large corporation and made the public aware of her fight. This burst of media coverage certainly led additional people to add their names to the petition, which totaled more than 40,000 signatures and ultimately prompted a response from Hasbro. Similarly, in the first 15 hours following Adam Lanza's murder spree at Sandy Hook elementary school, 100,000 digital signatures were added to a White House petition calling for stricter gun control laws. All of that seems quite impressive until we must consider that there are over 330 million people in the United States, and petitions supporting the cessation of Texas from the Union and the deportation of CNN host Piers Morgan also garnered more than 100,000 signatures. None of this is meant to dismiss the importance of the internet as a mobilizing structure for claims-makers, but rather point out that online technology allows frivolous matters to intersect with legitimate issues of public concern. In all probability, nobody is going to organize a claims-making campaign to prevent the deportation of Piers Morgan, yet inconsequential online petitions exist side-by-side with, and sometimes obtain a bigger response than matters like gun control, human rights, and other public policy matters. Regardless of whether or not this hinders the effectiveness of the internet as a claims-making medium, it might indicate that claims-makers with less social power face greater difficulty prompting a resolute mobilized response than more established institutional lobbyists like the National Rifle Association (NRA), should their online efforts be lost in the mass of competing claims flowing through cyberspace at any given time, or be delegitimized as representing insignificant issues that do not merit a serious response from policymakers (see Maratea, 2014).

Cause marketing and breast cancer awareness

When commodified through popular culture, the meanings associated with a particular social problem become manifested into products for general consumption. This approach is a part of a larger trend in how we combat social concerns referred to as *cause marketing*, which occurs when for-profit companies seeking to generate revenue or public goodwill align with non-profit enterprises looking to increase fundraising and social awareness. The goal is to brand social problems in commonsense ways that inspire emotional connections and mobilized action in consumers, while delivering financial benefits for corporate partners.

To better understand how cause marketing works to commodify social problems, consider how the pink ribbon has become the symbol of breast cancer as a social problem. Ribbons have a long history as a symbol through which people can show support for a cause, or spread a particular message about a social issue. The yellow ribbon, for instance, was widely adopted as a show of support among Americans during the Iran hostage crisis from 1979 to 1981, as well as the 1991 Gulf War. In a study of war-related ribbons, sociologist Terry Lilley and his colleagues note, "Collective displays of yellow ribbons during the first Gulf War were used to achieve a sense of community and to transmit identity in the form of a general support of troops." The idea is that, "Yellow ribbons not only *indicated* support for the troops, but they also symbolically *provided* that support" (Lilley et al, 2010: 313, emphasis in original). It is this very sense of solidarity and unity that has facilitated the proliferation of awareness ribbons for everything from energy in Nigeria (orange ribbon) to epilepsy (lavender), and even periwinkle ribbons for eating disorders, pulmonary hypertension, and craniofacial skull deformities. Some awareness ribbons, however, are more recognizable than others. HIV/AIDS awareness is represented by a red ribbon that was introduced in 1991, as "not a spontaneous phenomenon but a product conceived, produced, and marketed in the wake of the yellow ribbon's success as symbol" (Lilley et al, 2010: 314). 9/11 victims are commemorated with a black ribbon. During the 2003 Iraq War, magnetic "Support the Troops" ribbons were first manufactured for mass consumption, and then there is the eponymous pink-colored breast cancer awareness ribbon.

First created in 1991, by Charlotte Haley, the earliest breast cancer ribbons were actually peach in color. Hoping to get others to join the "grass roots movement" for greater breast cancer awareness, Haley affixed a note to the ribbons she sold that read: "The National Cancer

Institute's annual budget is $1.8 billion, only 5 percent goes for cancer prevention. Help us wake up legislators and America by wearing this ribbon." Haley's singlehanded efforts to marshal public support caught the attention of Alexandra Penney (then editor-in-chief of *Self* magazine) and Evelyn Lauder (of the Estée Lauder cosmetics company), who had hoped to use the peach ribbon to promote breast cancer awareness. When Haley declined to collaborate out of fear that Penney and Lauder would commercialize her peach ribbon, the ribbon's color was changed to pink and it soon became the recognizable symbol of breast cancer. By 1993, more than 1.5 million pink ribbons had been distributed at Estée Lauder makeup counters across the country (see Fernandez, 1998).

In retrospect, Haley's fears were prophetic. Over the past several decades, corporate philanthropy has become one of the driving forces of the breast cancer movement, using cause marketing to attract female consumers and raise funds for charitable organizations like Susan G. Komen (formerly Susan G. Komen for the Cure), the largest global non-profit advocating for breast cancer research (see King, 2010). Founded in 1982, by Nancy Brinker following the death of her sister (Susan Komen), the foundation has raised billions of dollars and helped direct public and political attention toward breast cancer awareness and research. However, much of Komen's influence can be attributed to its effective integration of cause marketing in its efforts, which has led critics to condemn the group's corporate-friendly approach to activism. While it is true Komen has raised millions of dollars for cancer research thanks to its Race for the Cure, a 5K nationwide run that Komen advertises as "the world's largest and most successful education and fundraising event for breast cancer ever created" (see http://apps.komen.org/raceforthecure/), as well as numerous cause-marketing campaigns, corporatized activism often frames the disease in ways that have more to do with encouraging customers to buy products than truly promoting breast cancer awareness.

According to Samantha King (2010), what results are manufactured human-interest narratives about survivorship that are beneficial to corporate and political actors but do little to advance public understanding of the disease, its risk factors, and what actually must be done to lower prevalence rates. "On the one hand breast cancer survivors are celebrated for their courage and strength and urged to feel empowered as actors within the medical system, but on the other they are asked to submit to mainstream scientific knowledge and depend on doctors and scientists to protect them from death. They – and the public at large – are told to obtain regular screenings, to demand insurance coverage for mammograms, and to explore a range of treatment options, but they are discouraged from questioning the underlying structures and guiding assumptions of the cancer-industrial complex," advanced through cause-marketing partnerships between activist groups and corporate entities (2010: 105).

The monetary and symbolic value associated with corporatized cause marketing is evident in the partnership between the National Football League (NFL), Komen, and the American Cancer Society. Since 2008, they have joined to promote the "A Crucial Catch" campaign to highlight the importance of regular breast cancer screenings.

> Throughout October, NFL games will feature players, coaches, and referees wearing pink game apparel, as well as additional on-field and in-stadium branding – all to help raise awareness for this important campaign. Much of the apparel worn at games by players and coaches, along with special game balls and pink coins, will be auctioned off at NFL Auction, with proceeds benefiting the American Cancer Society's Community Health Advocates implementing Nationwide Grants for Empowerment and Equity (CHANGE) program. (NFL, 2016)

Cause marketing, then, provides both a source of revenue for the NFL and invaluable branding for breast cancer activists. Of course, the use of cause marketing to symbolize concern for breast cancer extends to other corporate sponsors beyond the NFL. A trip to the grocery store can reveal all sorts of pink-themed products. In the past, Swiffer has sold limited edition pink kitchen mops. M&M candies have occasionally featured pink among their color mix. Similarly, in 2014, 5-Hour Energy released bottles of its pink lemonade-flavored energy drink, specially marked with a breast cancer awareness ribbon, and donated a portion of sale profits to charity. The list goes on and on even outside of grocery stores. Ford Motor Company has offered special edition vehicles with pink accessories and gun manufacturer Smith & Wesson marketed a handgun replete with a pink pistol grip with an engraved ribbon.

Although each of these partnerships provides important notoriety and a source of fundraising for breast cancer advocacy groups, there are many concerns about the blatant synergizing of corporate interests and issue advocacy. From a moral or ethical standpoint, we must consider whether advocacy groups committed to curing social ills should be aligning themselves with businesses seeking to use social problems as a source of financial gain. For example, numerous companies that market under the auspices of the pink ribbon campaign produce products that are known to increase the risk of breast cancer. The advocacy group Breast Cancer Action even coined the term "pinkwashing" to refer to "a company or organization that claims to care about breast cancer by promoting a pink ribbon product, but at the same time produces, manufactures and/or sells products that are linked to the disease" (Breast Cancer Action, 2016). In 2010, for example, Susan G. Komen was criticized for partnering with Kentucky Fried Chicken (KFC) for the "Buckets for a Cure" campaign, during which traditional white serving buckets were replaced with pink ones. The problem for critics was that unhealthy fast foods like those sold at KFC have been found to increase the risk of breast cancer among women. At the same time, however, the pink bucket campaign alone raised millions of dollars of much needed funding for Komen; and the sheer glut of pink products on the marketplace at any given time is testament to the need for corporate partnerships and their value in raising awareness to social problems like breast cancer.

Box 6.3: Pinkwashing

Marketing social problems can result in a synergistic relationship between issue advocates and corporations that offers mutual benefits to both parties – issue advocates gain much needed visibility and resources, while corporations often benefit from the public good will generated by their close ties to a favored social cause. Critics contend, however, that such relationships are fraught with challenges and may actually undermine efforts to understand and combat social issues. One example of such criticisms can be seen in the "Think Before You Pink" campaign carried out by Breast Cancer Action (BCA). BCA is an organization that began in 2002 in response to concerns about the rapidly increasing number of pink ribbon products on the market. At the heart of BCA's concerns is a belief that the issue of breast cancer has been framed almost entirely as a matter of individual risk and individual solutions (eg self-screening and mammography) rather than as a systemic problem that demands institutional and cultural change. BCA's contention is the various pink campaigns have become more about symbolic politics than substantive change. In other words, they believe that the use of pink ribbons has become so widespread that it has become meaningless in many instances. As they note, "Any company can put the pink ribbon on any product, regardless of how much money – if any – goes to breast cancer." Moreover, they argue that some of these companies and organizations are guilty of *pinkwashing*, a term that refers to the practices of companies that claim to care about breast cancer by promoting a variety of pink ribbon products while they also manufacture and sell products that are linked to the disease, such as automobiles, fast food, and cosmetics (see King, 2008).

Clearly, cause marketing can help brand a social problem for public consumption. Breast cancer went from being a largely ignored or misunderstood problem to one that has enjoyed more than two decades of sustained visibility, in large part due to the pink ribbon campaign and effective use of corporate alignments. Despite these successes, Barbara Brenner, executive director of Breast Cancer Action, expressed skepticism of cause marketing in a 2010 NPR interview, noting, "If shopping could cure breast cancer, it would be cured by now" (National Public Radio, 2010). Her point is simple – the touted benefits of cause marketing can be misleading and at times downright deceptive. Often it is unclear how much money tied to a purchase is actually redirected to charity, who gets the money, or how the money is used. Case in point, the NFL does donate 90% of its royalty share (25%) from the wholesale price of pink merchandise sold during the "A Crucial Catch" campaign to the American Cancer Society, but that equates to just $11.25 out of every $100. Of that total, approximately 70% is donated to promoting cancer screenings, but none to cancer research. All told, the NFL has donated just under $8 million since partnering with the American Cancer Society in 2008, but this pales in comparison to the $10 billion the league made in revenue during 2014 alone (see Sinha, 2014; Notte, 2015). None of this is to say the American Cancer Society should be unhappy with the arrangement. For one month every year the NFL provides priceless advertising for breast cancer awareness to fans of the most popular professional sport in the United States; and these efforts may very well trigger additional resource mobilization among people who are inspired by the NFL's campaign to donate their own time or money to help fight cancer. After all, more than anything else, cause marketing is intended to brand a social problem so that it becomes more recognizable to the larger population of would-be advocates who are needed to supply the symbolic (eg support) and material (eg donations) resources needed for claimants to subsidize their ongoing campaigns for social change.

The socio-political foundations of cause marketing

At this point, it is useful to ask why breast cancer, ALS, and other social problems must be advertised to the public, and why people are more likely to mobilize support after seeing NFL players wearing pink, or videos of celebrities dumping ice cold water on their heads. In many ways, the necessity of cause marketing for claims-makers and issue advocates is rooted in the complexities of modern life. Back in 1981, President Ronald Reagan articulated the vision behind cause marketing when he noted in a speech that philanthropy helps generate "economic incentives and investment opportunities," because "America's deep spirit of generosity" stimulates commercial ventures that can help "solve our social ills (Reagan, 1981). While there is some truth to Reagan's sentiment, just how genuine are efforts to address social problems when some of the involved parties are expecting to profit financially? It is reasonable, for instance, to question whether the NFL would be so willing to promote breast cancer awareness if the league did not accrue millions in revenue selling pink merchandise each year. Furthermore, there are practical limits to our collective "deep spirit of generosity," making it impossible to adequately fund all of the efforts being made at a given time to identify and cure social problems. Most people simply have very little available *surplus compassion*, which refers to the time, energy, and resources we can allocate to social issues above and beyond the concerns of our own everyday lives. Amidst the hustle and bustle of our daily routines and with so many people struggling just to make ends meet (and so many different social problems constantly being advertised to us), it often becomes difficult to dedicate sufficient consideration to social causes that don't directly harm you or a loved one. In other words, when we donate time or money to fight social problems like ALS, or climate change, it inevitably means we have fewer resources to allocate for other concerns like animal welfare and marriage equality.

You can be sure that claims-makers are aware of this fact, and this is precisely why advertising themselves and their chosen social problems to the public is so important. Compounding matters is the fact that the press has neither the time nor the resources to report on every available story about prospective social problems, meaning news workers must focus their attention on matters that are particularly newsworthy, engaging, and can be cost effectively relayed to audiences. Claimants seeking recognition must therefore frame their issues and efforts in ways that are compelling enough to attract media coverage – think of marches, public rallies, or acts of civil disobedience, such as women's right supporters burning their bras and Vietnam war protesters destroying their draft cards during the 1960s – that will spread the word to supportive individuals and groups with sufficient financial resources to subsidize their advocacy. Sociologists John D. McCarthy and Mayer N. Zald (1977) refer to this as the process of *resource mobilization*, which explains how, when, and why claimants acquire the symbolic (such as news coverage) and material (money, volunteer labor, and so forth) capital needed to remain solvent, extend their social reach, and accomplish their goals. One of the most effective ways activists draw attention to themselves and the social problems they seek to expose is by exploiting a *discourse of fear* to scare the public into believing a social problem exists that threatens their welfare (see Altheide, 2002). In doing so, claimants might put forth gross mischaracterizations of the etiology, extent, and nature of a given social ill, yet these patterned misrepresentations tend to validate a social problem's existence because they often align with mainstream ideologies that are shaped by the narratives disseminated by news and entertainment media, politicians and other public figures, and the corporate entities that strongly influence popular perceptions about social issues (Sacco, 2005; Maratea and Monahan, 2013). After all, claims-makers are a lot like a sales person in any other business – they are not obligated to tell you the truth in order to sell you their product, or problem.

Symbolic communities: seeking solidarity through popular culture

Regardless of whether claims-making efforts are genuinely truthful or blur the lines of reality, the commodification of social problems is always intended to inspire a supportive response through branding that can be recognized publicly by wearing pink NFL jerseys, sporting color-coded wristbands, placing a bumper sticker on a car, or even tweeting a trending hashtag. Yet popular culture is more than a marketing vehicle; it is also a platform for displaying unity because the products produced when social problems are commodified become symbolic markers of affiliation to a cause. Think about going to a sporting event and seeing all of the fans around you wearing apparel that signifies what team they are rooting for that day. The decision to adorn oneself with symbols that represent a particular group of athletes, such as the team's logo, colors, and so forth, serves as declaration of one's allegiances to others in the audience. The same basic principles apply when someone elects to associate themselves with identifiers of a social cause.

We can see collective concerns coalesce around social problems in the form of symbolic actions when lots of people apply the same colored theme to their Facebook profile photo in recognition of a social problem, tweet a hashtag like *#blacklivesmatter*, or shave their heads in solidarity with a cancer patient. Most of the time, however, communities of support develop from a combination of commercial and symbolic efforts. One example of this can be seen in the yellow wristbands associated with the

The Colour Run: an example of commodification and symbolic communities

© Sean Gao: http://www.istockphoto.com/gb/photo/runners-photographing-before-color-run-2012-gm458881859-23501049?st=_p_23501049

well-known "Livestrong" campaign, first established by Lance Armstrong in 1996, after he had been diagnosed with testicular cancer. At the time, a prominent American competitive cyclist, Armstrong used his fame and public visibility as catalysts in founding the Lance Armstrong Foundation (now known as the Livestrong Foundation) in 1997, a non-profit charitable organization providing support, resources, and advocating for public policy initiatives that improve the lives of people affected by cancer.

Thanks in no small part to Armstrong's celebrity and presence as a public symbol of resilience, strength, and perseverance in fighting a disease that personally affects so many people, the Livestrong Foundation had a competitive advantage over other fledgling activist organizations similarly seeking social and political recognition. But it was not until 2004, that the publicity breakthrough occurred that would change how the American public displayed their symbolic opposition to cancer – the introduction of the yellow Livestrong bracelet. It quickly became one of the more ubiquitous popular culture items of the early 2000s, with more than 70 million sold in the first three years after it was introduced (Ruibal, 2007).

But few knew it was developed by Nike's advertising agency as a fundraising item, and much like colored ribbons, the yellow wristband spurred an entire cottage industry of similarly designed awareness bracelets for seemingly every malady in existence. This includes satirist Stephen Colbert's red Wriststrong bracelets, humorously intended to recognize the seriousness of wrist injuries after Colbert had suffered an injury on the set of *The Colbert Report* in 2008. In actuality, and perhaps unbeknownst to some of the people who purchased a Wriststrong bracelet, all profits from its sales were donated to The Yellow Ribbon Fund, which provides services to American soldiers injured during active duty. Similar to Lance Armstrong providing the public visibility that catapulted the Livestrong bracelet trend, Colbert's celebrity status allowed him to market satire to the public and use it to raise funds for a very serious charitable organization, even though it is reasonable to conclude that many of the people who donated by purchasing a Wriststrong bracelet were oblivious to the actual cause they were supporting!

The previously discussed ice bucket challenge offers yet another example of the convergence of popular culture with symbolic and material resource mobilization. An entertaining and lighthearted marketing gimmick that did not focus on the horrors and sadness of a disease with no cure, the ice bucket challenge used popular culture as a vehicle to prompt public participation. Whether people connected with the issue through direct (by publishing videos dumping water on themselves or donating money) or indirect (by watching news reports or clips of people taking the ice bucket challenge) action, the success of the ice bucket challenge was not the result of people en masse taking to the streets and protesting for the immediate cure of a terrible disease. It was instead reflective of the ice bucket challenge's commodification of a social problem through mass marketing. Many people were essentially buying into a trend distributed to them via popular culture. In other words, they were responding to the gimmick, which in turn generated a secondary awareness to the underlying social problem and helped crystallize a community of support made publicly visible through all of the videos uploaded by people who accepted the challenge and dumped water on their heads. This, in turn, prompted a redirection of public attention and financial resources toward ALS research.

It is not uncommon to see similar public displays of support (or opposition) in the fight against all sorts of other prospective social problems. Consider the global reaction to the terrorist shooting at the headquarters of the French satirical magazine *Charlie Hebdo* on January 7, 2015, which left 11 people dead and prompted millions of French citizens to participate in unity rallies across the country. Globally the slogan "*Je suis Charlie*" (which translates to "I am Charlie") became a rallying cry of solidarity and resistance in the fight against terrorism and to uphold the democratic ideals of freedom of speech. We saw a similar collective response to the November 2015 terrorist bombings in Paris, after which millions of Facebook users exploited their social media presence to publicly display their solidarity by superimposing the colors of the French flag over their profile photos. Interestingly, there was no comparable show of support for the people of Mali after gunmen murdered 27 people in a Radisson hotel in an apparent terrorist act just days after the attacks in Paris.

While it can be argued the scale and scope of the Paris bombings exceeded the massacre in Mali, the diverging responses suggest that when prompted via popular culture, people are selective in publicly identifying with causes and social problems. After all, there were no catchphrases or hashtags that went viral to commemorate the Mali shootings, and news coverage of that attack was comparably less than either the *Charlie Hebdo* or Paris bombing incidents; and social media outlets like Facebook failed to offer users the opportunity to superimpose the colors of Mali over their Facebook photos as they did in solidarity with the French. What this suggests is that communities of support do not objectively emerge in response to social problems. Rather, individual and collective decisions to express unity and display symbolic resistance to a social scourge depends in large part on where those particular problems are located within the hierarchy of our normative value structures. For instance, terrorism tends to hold a prominent place in the collective conscience of citizens in the westernized world, which is why violent attacks so commonly inspire very emotional and public displays of solidarity. Examples include the prominent displaying of American flags following 9/11; mourners holding candlelight vigils in memory of victims; people adopting the "Boston Strong" slogan following the 2013 marathon bombing; and supporters attending either gun rights or gun control rallies following a mass shooting. Regardless of whether these collective efforts are intended to support the status quo (eg displays of nationalism) or pushback against a perceived harm to the social order (eg fighting injustice), the sense of resistance through shared beliefs that emerges from membership in a symbolic community may help cultivate a sense of empowerment and self-determination among participants who, as distinct individuals, are relatively powerless to affect social change, but when banded together may come to believe they are fighting for their vision of a more perfect world.

Conclusion

Oftentimes, popular culture is the crux around which symbolic communities of support evolve in response to successfully marketed social problems. This is partly because publicly branded social problems are readily identifiable when advertised using wristbands, slogans, clothing, music, or any other material or symbolic gesture intended to communicate opposition or support for a particular issue. These commodities can emerge as important markers that symbolize solidarity in much the same way that displaying a lawn sign or campaign button demonstrates allegiance to a political candidate during an election. The problem, however, is that while these marketable commodities help raise money and awareness, they also tend to commercialize social problems in a way that can ultimately marginalize communities of support over time.

In the conclusion of Chapter Five it was noted how hip-hop and rap music have been adopted as forms of *pushback* against dominant social norms. As artistic genres, hip-hop and rap have been and continue to be important vehicles for symbolic resistance to social problems like racism, sexism, patriarchy, and colonialism. But their immense popularity has also rendered them very valuable as economic commodities, and this has led to increasing commercialization of the form by corporate actors and others whose efforts often undermine, sanitize, or simply dilute messages of pushback against the status quo.

> Corporate America's infatuation with rap has increased as the genre's political content has withered. Ice Cube's early songs attacked white racism; Ice-T sang a song about a cop killer; Public Enemy challenged listeners to "fight the power". But many newer acts are focused almost entirely on pathologies within the black community. They rap about shooting other blacks, but almost never about challenging governmental authority or encouraging social activism. (Farley, 1999)

Through commercialization, the popularity and notoriety of hip-hop has diffused to suburban and white audiences, and there has been a corresponding rise in bureaucratic narratives co-opting the genre through claims that reflect the dominant order of white society. Most commonly distributed through mainstream media, these claims characterize hip-hop as reflecting all of the stereotypical social ills pervading African-American youth and communities, such as hyper-violent behaviors, misogyny, and lack of personal responsibility; and they frame *black culture* as the root cause of social problems that harm the black community. What this suggests is that popular culture can shape and then reshape the way social problems are marketed to the public in order to endorse or delegitimize pushback efforts.

The reality that institutional, corporate, and bureaucratic actors with considerable power in the public sphere can manipulate social narratives so that messages of resistance can be commercialized as a source of profit and conformity to mainstream culture is a fundamentally important point. Selling social problems is a lot like marketing any other commercial product. Just as an effective advertisement piques consumer interest in an attempt to increase sales, successful claimants convince the public to buy into their espoused concerns in hopes of mobilizing their physical, financial, and symbolic support. But there are profound consequences to selling social problems to audiences through material goods, and we should consider critically whether it really helps to solve those problems.

Commodification can certainly provide people with a sense of participation and accomplishment that they have done something to combat a social problem. However, commodification may only cultivate superficial commitments from supporters who need only wear a wristband or buy a t-shirt to feel like they are doing something meaningful to advance their chosen cause. Yet these sorts of efforts only confirm that people are willing to partake in a relatively shallow form of mobilized action, which requires little or no industry on their part.

In many ways, these sorts of symbolic and material investments are important because they reflect shared beliefs and can help to build and reinforce a communal sense of collective identity or belief among likeminded thinkers (see DiMaggio et al, 2001; Nip, 2004). Building and reinforcing these relationships are vital when combatting a social problem since they represent the formation of *weak ties* that are "indispensable to individuals' ... integration into communities" because they bind together populations whose interpersonal relations would otherwise be nonexistent or lacking in mutual intensity and intimacy (Granovetter, 1973: 1378). The problem, however, is these social ties may not be strong enough to sustain individual and collective interest for a long enough time to actually make significant progress in solving the social problem. This is because people may have a tendency to mobilize against social problems only after they become commodified fads – think of how the ice bucket challenge and yellow Livestrong bracelets burst into cultural relevance – but do not sustain their interest and investment once those fads dissipate. Furthermore, to the extent that people feel like they have done their part to solve a social problem simply by purchasing a commodified good or displaying a symbolic marker, then they can move on with their lives as if the problem has been solved, when in fact that very ill might be ongoing and at risk of losing cultural relevance as public attention shifts to the latest and greatest commodified problem.

At the end of the day we must remember that the social problems process is, at its core, about the construction of social meanings. Although we might like to believe the meanings we attach to social problems and the symbolic communities that we choose to align ourselves with are the product of our own independent judgments, the truth is, we all are influenced by the claims, narratives, and frames that we consume through popular culture, many of which are intended to cultivate compliance and minimize resistance. This is why it is important to recognize the marketing of social problems, and our membership in symbolic communities are never entirely removed from the prevailing power structure, which can manipulate popular culture as a diffusive and insidious instrument of coercion.

KEY QUESTIONS

What is commodification with respect to social problems? How does it influence if and how social problems are delivered to the public?

What is cause marketing? What are some ways that it affects the social problems process?

Are there any categories of goods that tend to feature more in cause marketing? Why or why not? Do these efforts seem to be directed more towards some categories than other (eg, gender, age, occupation, and so on)? Why or why not?

Look through your own personal effects (clothing, jewelry, and so on) for evidence of cause marketing. Can you identify any items that reveal a connection between you and a symbolic community? If so, how do you think having such items shapes your view of the issues around which that symbolic community is formed?

SUGGESTED READINGS

King, S. (2006) *Pink Ribbons, Inc.: Breast cancer and the politics of philanthropy*, Minneapolis, MN: University of Minnesota Press.

Penney, J. (2015) "Social media and symbolic action: exploring participation in the Facebook red equal sign profile picture campaign", *Journal of Computer-Mediated Interaction*, 20(1):52-66.

Richey, L.A. and Ponte, S. (2011) *Brand Aid: Shopping well to save the world*, Minneapolis, MN: University of Minnesota Press.

SEVEN

Conclusion

Throughout this book we have attempted to describe how and why popular culture influences our individual and collective understandings of the social problems that people come to believe exist in our world. Our main premise is that popular culture is an important vehicle through which social problems are constructed and sold to the public by claims-makers. After all, it is important to recognize that social problems do not just emerge out of thin air like a magician pulling a rabbit out of a hat. They are instead readily connected by claims-makers to demonstrable indicators of their existence, risks, and potential harms. Yet for these indicators to be identified and connected to a particular issue in ways that generate collective fear, claimants have to generate compelling claims that can be circulated for mass consumption in the public sphere. This is because social problems do not necessarily reflect the objective existence of harmful conditions in society. Rather, social problems become collectively recognized through the efforts of politicians, journalists, and other influential claims-makers as they repeatedly tell the public that a particular harm threatens society and their personal welfare. As Joel Best (2013) suggests, "It is not an objective quality of a social condition, but rather the subjective reactions to that condition, that make something a social problem. Therefore, social problems should not be viewed as a type of social condition, but as a *process* of responding to social conditions" (2013: 9-10, emphasis in original).

Sometimes the harm posed by a social problem is so clear and convincing that there is a general public consensus about its existence. For instance, most Americans agree that Al Qaeda was responsible for the terrorist attacks of 9/11, even though a small number of "truthers" dispute this fact and instead argue the US Government staged the strikes in order to curtail civil liberties and build a coalition of support for wars in Iraq and Afghanistan (see Manjoo, 2006). Violent crimes that occur in public spaces, like mass shootings, and natural disasters similarly produce visible carnage and storylines of victimization that may evoke among audiences a shared sense of trauma, destruction, and impending doom. At other times, however, it is less clear whether the issues presented to us as social problems are really as catastrophic as they are made to seem. Watch television news on any given night and you might be told that everything from driving on highways to malfunctioning escalators and risqué clothing styles are scary epidemics that everyone should fear. Now there might not be enough *actual* harm resulting from these supposed problems to justify public concern. But so long as enough people respond to those media reports and evoke a sense of panic, it becomes increasingly likely that things like faulty escalators and road rage will draw the continued attention of claims-makers, news workers, and elected officials vowing to rectify the scourge. In Chapter Three we examined this very point when discussing the prevalence of news coverage dedicated to protecting children from Halloween sadism. Every October parents are reminded that countless children fall victim to candy that has been poisoned or tainted with razor blades. But in reality, the dangers of contaminated Halloween candy are nothing more than an urban legend that thrives because of its annually recurring cultural relevance and connection to existing generalized fears about child endangerment (see Best and Horiuchi, 1985; Best, 1990; Zelizer, 1994). The point is that there often exists a gap between that *actual* harm caused by a social threat and the *perception* of harm it generates among the public, the press, and policymakers.

Popular culture is without question part of the reason this gap exists because it helps to shape (and sensationalize) our individual and collective perceptions of what is a social problem, and how we should respond to those fears. As we have discussed throughout the book, there are common linkages between popular culture and the social problems process – *blaming*, *spreading*, *pushback*, and *marketing* – that each reflect varying motivations and strategies for raising public awareness. For instance, some might see popular culture as a means of promoting an ideology (spreading), while others might use it to reinforce an established claim (blaming), package counterclaims that challenge common beliefs (pushback), or mobilize resources (marketing). Collectively, these linkages underscore the fact that popular culture is a valuable resource for claims-makers to build, bolster, and disseminate their claims; yet none of them simply exist waiting to be discovered. Instead, claims-makers and other social actors must actively cultivate these linkages if they are to obtain *ownership* of a social problem; that is, become the primary definers of the issue.

> By assuming ownership ... a movement applies its ideology to establish an authoritative interpretation, reducing the cacophony of competing interpretations in favor of one dominant view promoted by the movement... A movement's assuming ownership of a new ... problem markedly improves the chances of [it] being institutionalized, but also enhances the movement's long term prospects. (Best, 1999: 64–5)

When claims-makers succeed in obtaining ownership of a problem, they command the social authority to visibly promote their cause in a way that piques continued media coverage and increases the likelihood that public officials will address the concern, which gives them a distinct competitive advantage over other activists offering alternative perspectives.

The infusion of popular culture with claims-making operations helps activists distribute claims that are varied and novel – both of which are essential if claimants hope to maintain public interest in their social problem. The value of pop culture in this regard stems from the fact that it is deeply intertwined in everyday life for most people. Social problem scholars have long noted that claimants need to acquire and maintain sufficient resources to commence and navigate a successful claims-making campaign (Best, 2013). Generally, activism is an expensive and time-consuming process that requires both a great deal of organization and sufficient financial resources; many claims-makers simply lack the available assets needed to discredit opponents and sustain operations through to completion (see McCarthy and Zald, 1977). Yet from a social problems perspective, resources can go well beyond financial value. For instance, some things offer visible symbolic value, such as a charismatic spokesperson or celebrity endorser, child victims, wounded animals, suffering military troops, and even first responders after 9/11. Symbolic resources are important because they influence how people process information, relate to individuals' experiences, reinforce (and sometimes challenge) morality, invite sympathetic responses, increase public visibility, and evoke strong emotional reactions that resonate among audiences who feel they have a vested interest in a problem's solution (see Graber, 1988; Best, 1990; Loseke, 2003). Symbolic resources, then, help claimants – including those with relatively little social capital at their disposal – to institutionalize their issues and perspectives as credible, in the minds of news workers, policymakers, and the general public.

Another reason that popular culture is an effective way to spread claims is the subtle insidiousness to the integration of claims making and activism with pop culture. That is, most people do not necessarily interact with popular culture for the express purpose of learning about and responding to social problems, meaning claimants have the opportunity to connect with audience members when their guards are down and they might not be thinking critically about social problems and the messages they are receiving. After all, if you are preparing to root for your team in a big game, you might not be thinking of the implications of *paid patriotism* and governmental efforts to promote pro-war propaganda to a public that is divided on the necessity of US global military intervention (the same would be true if anti-war groups sponsored *paid pacifist* propaganda during sporting events). The fact is, popular culture pervades social life and defines the commercial materialism that characterizes westernized societies; and through it we not only consume material products but also the perspectives, ideals, and beliefs of those people and groups with the social power to transmit their claims to audiences in the public sphere.

Popular culture exists as a point of commonality shared by people with diverging interests, ideologies, and beliefs in a given society, making it an extremely powerful medium for claimants to connect with broad audiences. With regards to the construction of social problems, this fact is important because popular culture ties each of us as individuals to the larger collective, whether through our fashion styles, musical preferences, need for the latest smart phone, or more generally, by our participation in fads and trends. Consequently, when claimants strategically immerse claims-making practices within popular culture, they are attempting to elicit a strong emotional response that attracts journalistic attention and rallies populist support. As sociologist Joel Best (1990) notes, claims-makers want to "make everyone in the audience feel that he or she has a vested interest in the problem's solution," and by couching claims within popular culture, they have the ability to characterize "a problem in terms of an individual's experiences" so that they resonate as relevant and are easier to comprehend (1990: 31, 41). In other words, invoking popular cultural dialogues, processes, and products better positions claimants to frame the social problems they are selling to the public in ways that news workers, audiences, and policymakers find plausible.

The simple fact is that claims-makers connect with you (and the broader public) through popular culture because popular culture is conduit through which we all connect with the social world. This is precisely why it is so important to recognize how, when, and why popular culture influences so much more than the television shows you watch, music you listen to, and clothes that you wear. Culture is essentially a lens that directs our attention to the fads, fashions, trends, commodities, and issues that we are socialized to desire, lust, loathe, or fear. But it only functions in this capacity because claims-makers, activists, journalists, business leaders, bureaucrats, and other influential people and groups make concerted efforts to manipulate culture so that their preferred definitions and meanings about social issues (politics, economics, social problems, etc) are transmitted to the public in ways that generate a collective response (fear, anger, calls for action, and so forth). Some activists may use popular culture to push back against dominant and institutionalized understandings of social problems in order to reframe the narrative and usurp the power political and economic insiders. These are usually outsiders to the political process with relatively little social power, and therefore they face intense competition in getting their claims recognized, because they must first identify constituents, attract their attention through media exposure, win their support, and mobilize them into action. Others seek to preserve the status quo by co-opting popular culture in order to spread propaganda that represents the established political and economic order. This collection of insiders is comprised of powerful lobbying and pressure groups like the National Rifle Association (NRA), which have close ties to the policymaking process and therefore can advance their agendas directly to political and economic leaders but nonetheless pursue publicity generating clout-building campaigns designed to both monitor how the larger citizenry responds to their issues and remind legislators of their political sway (Best, 1990; 2008; Benford and Hunt, 2003). The distinction between insiders and outsiders is important because it suggests the playing field is tilted in favor of powerful claimants with established ties to political, economic, and social institutions because they "can routinely influence government decisions and can ensure that their interests are normally recognized in the decision-making process" (Useem and Zald, 1982: 144). Even though you will probably never see people protesting *in defense of* unpopular industries like coal and tobacco, you can be sure that the halls of Congress are jam -packed with lobbyists defending their interests.

This is precisely why understanding the role played by popular culture in the social problem process is so important; it provides a channel for competing factions – outsiders that challenge mainstream understandings of social problems and insiders who promote the interests of political and economic elites – to effectively engage in combative claims making with hopes of convincing you to support their positions.

We hope that all of the things discussed in the pages of this book have revealed an important (and perhaps scary) truth that the judgments we all reach about whether a particular social problem exists, and whether to support or oppose proposed solutions, never really materializes from your own independent analysis of those problems and their perceived harms. Although popular culture might sometimes seem as innocent as puppies and ice cream when you are watching your favorite movie or out shopping with friends, its entertaining and commercial veneer masks how it functions as such a powerfully coercive force in all of our lives.

The idea that popular culture diverts our attention from "the important stuff" through commercially produced mass entertainment continues to persist in public life (see Adorno, 1941; Horkheimer and Adorno, [1944] 2002; Grazian, 2010; Sellnow, 2014). Neil Postman, a renowned mass communications scholar, addressed this point in writing about the intersections of technology and culture. In his best-known book, *Amusing Ourselves to Death* (1985), he maintains that the emergence of television as a communication medium precipitated a significant decline in the quality of information delivered to the public and the overall character of public discourse. Television, he argues, "gives us a conversation in images, not words" (1985: 7), thereby removing so much of the depth and nuance found in other mediated and non-mediated forms of face-to-face, radio, and print communication. For Postman (1985), the chief quandary with television is the inherent artifices of its programs and personalities: "The problem is not that television presents us with entertaining subject matter but that all subject matter is presented as entertaining" (1985: 87).

Of course, the media industry has grown considerably since Postman first advanced these arguments. Over the last few decades television has been joined – and in many ways surpassed – by a host of new communication technologies, such as the expansion of cable and satellite television programming, digital devices like smart phones, and the internet, replete with an information superhighway full of social media, citizen journalism, and lots of other corporate, bureaucratic, and user-generated content. Farhad Manjoo (2008) argues that the sheer enormity of information available now gives individuals greater authority to seek out what they believe to be true regardless of whether their viewpoints are certifiably factual. As our individual and collective attention gets diverted among an increasing array of platforms and technologies that provide countless access points for incredibly fast entertainment and information retrieval, Manjoo suggests that truth no longer exists objectively, but is instead constructed from the "facts" that we choose to accept or ignore.

> No longer are we holding opinions different from one another; we're also holding different facts ... the creeping partisanship has begun to distort our very perceptions about what is "real" and what isn't. Indeed, you can go so far as to say we're now fighting over competing versions of reality. And it is more convenient than ever before for some of us to live in a world built out of our own facts. (Manjoo, 2008: 2)

For Manjoo, the seminal issue is the ease by which opinion can now be confirmed as fact, thereby allowing most anyone to become a lay expert by simply going out and finding information online that validates his or her beliefs, even if it contradicts established scientific truth about social problems or any other matter of public importance.

Both Postman and Manjoo essentially argue that public communication is symbiotically connected with the popular culture industry, and that we must remain mindful of how these forces shape our individual worldview. There is no escaping that popular culture influences how every reader of this book learns about and engages with a variety of social issues even if life experience, personality traits, and a whole host of factors unique to each individual, help explain why people interpret claims differently. This is precisely why people can watch a television show like *Breaking Bad* or a film like *Scarface* and some may find that they glorify drug dealing and violence, while others might see the harms of adopting criminal lifestyles, and still others might view them as little more than harmless fictional entertainment that will have no effect on its viewers' future behaviors. Still, the key is to remember that there are claims-makers out there actively attempting to use popular culture as a mechanism for shaping our thoughts, and influencing how we perceive the world around us, and this impacts much more than just our understanding of social problems. We see it when political candidates seeking the support of voters appear on television shows like *Saturday Night Live* and *The Daily Show*. We see it when businesses that want consumers to buy their goods hire a celebrity spokesperson and strategically place their products in your favorite movies. We see it when journalists present news in a sensationalized way that produces "infotainment," or the combining of current events with entertaining human-interest stories.

The Italian theorist and intellectual Antonio Gramsci (1891–1937) coined the term *cultural hegemony* to describe how the powerful dominant classes in society use mass culture and social institutions (political, economic, educational, religious, and so forth) to present a worldview that promotes their interests to the larger population in such a way that the values, beliefs, goals, and needs of the powerful are imposed on society as a whole. And because social and political elites control the flow of information through mass culture and social institutions, they are able to frame their worldview as beneficial to everyone so that over time it becomes the status quo and the only logical way of viewing the world. The vast majority of people who are largely powerless, then, come to support a mass culture and social order that neither truly benefits them nor promotes their collective interests (see Gramsci, 1971). Now scholars and students may debate the extent to which the concept of cultural hegemony accurately describes the ideological and practical functioning of modern society. However, the larger point is that relatively few people – whether they are politicians, corporate executives, religious leaders, lobbyists, activists, or any other sort of claims-maker – define the parameters of public discourse for the masses, and you can be sure that they are actively using popular culture to convince you to support their views, buy their products, or fear the social problem they are selling to the public.

Back in Chapter Two, we discussed how social theorists like Theodor Adorno and Max Horkheimer argue that culture molds public consciousness by coercing citizens to passively acquiesce to the dominant authority of political and corporate actors and institutions who direct our collective focus towards all of the mass-produced goods that we want (but do not necessarily need), which prevents us from seeing that we have become slaves to the social control of materialism, consumerism, and mainstream conformity. We have also attempted to show that popular culture can also function as a vehicle for challenging the status quo by reframing social problems and establishing and legitimizing alternative meanings that may fundamentally change mainstream understandings of those issues. In doing so, we hope that you have come to see that claims-makers are constantly attempting to sell you social problems in much the same way that a store clerk might try to sell you a car or new television. The difference, of course, is that claimants want you to buy their ideas, values, meanings, and beliefs, instead of a material product (although they might sell you material products like shirts and wristbands, so that you symbolically advertise your agreement with their ideas, values, meanings, and beliefs). Yet whether you are in the market for a new cause to support, or smartphone to purchase, the people selling them to you are relying on you being responsive to their sales pitch.

In many ways, claimants do not necessarily care whether we are young or old, liberal or conservative, men or women, black or white, so long as they can orient our perceptions toward their worldview and inspire us to donate monetary and symbolic resources. Regardless of whether we notice the role that popular culture plays in accomplishing this goal, we hope this book has helped reveal how and why popular culture exists as a mechanism of social control. We also hope that you think critically about how your life intersects with popular culture and not commit blindly to the idea that pop culture is nothing more than harmless fads and trends because it may prevent you from seeing all the ways culture and technology can influence our lives if we are not paying attention.

References

AFP (2016) "Hashtag Fail? #BringBackOurGirls two years on, and the limits of keyboard activism", *Mail & Guardian Africa*, April 13. Available at: http://mgafrica.com/article/2016-04-13-hashtag-fail-bringbackourgirls-two-years-on [Retrieved April 13, 2016].

Adorno, T.W. (1941) "On popular music", *Studies in Philosophy and Social Science*, 9: 17-48.

Adorno, T.W. (2001) *The culture industry: Selected essays on mass culture* (2nd edn), New York, NY: Routledge.

Adorno, T.W. (2006) "On popular music", in J. Storey (ed) *Cultural theory and popular culture: A reader* (3rd edn), New York, NY: Pearson, pp 73-84.

Altheide, D.L. (1995) *An ecology of communication: Cultural formats of control.* Hawthorne, NY: Aldine de Gruyter.

Altheide, D.L. (2002) *Creating fear: News and the construction of crisis.* Hawthorne, NY: Aldine de Gruyter.

Alter, C. (2014) "The problem with pit bulls", *Time*, June 20. Available at: http://time.com/2891180/kfc-and-the-pit-bull-attack-of-a-little-girl/ [Retrieved January 5, 2016].

Amira, D. (2013) "The least suspicious person since roof man is 'Running Away Man'", *New York Magazine*, April 17. Available at: http://nymag.com/daily/intelligencer/2013/04/running-away-man-not-suspicious-photos.html [Retrieved December 8, 2015].

Appelo, T. (2012) "THR poll: 'Glee' and 'Modern Family' drive voters to favor gay marriage – even many Romney voters", *The Hollywood Reporter*, November 3. Available at: http://www.hollywoodreporter.com/news/thr-poll-glee-modern-family-386225 [Retrieved December 16, 2015].

Associated Press (2006) "WHO: Bird flu poses bigger challenge than AIDS", *Fox News*, March 6. Available at: http://www.foxnews.com/story/0,2933,186974,00.html [Retrieved April 14, 2008].

Associated Press (2009) "Richard Allen Samuel McCroskey III, suspect in 4 killings, rapped about thrill of murder", *New York Daily News*, September 20. Available at: http://www.nydailynews.com/news/national/richard-allen-samuel-mccroskey-iii-suspect-4-killings-rapped-thrill-murder-article-1.406054 [Retrieved February 18, 2015].

Austerlitz, S. (2014) *Sitcom: A history in 24 episodes from I Love Lucy to community*, Chicago, IL: Chicago Review Press.

Ayanbadejo, B. (2014) "Coming out a liberating move for Michael Sam", *Fox Sports*, February 9. Available at: http://www.foxsports.com/nfl/story/ayanbadejo-coming-out-a-liberating-move-for-michael-sam-020914 [Retrieved December 1, 2015].

Baer, J. and Chambliss, W.J. (1997) "Generating fear: the politics of crime reporting", *Crime, Law & Social Change*, 27: 87-107.

Baier, B. (2012) "What President Obama really said in that '60 Minutes' interview about Benghazi", *Fox News*, November 5. Available at: http://politics.blogs.foxnews.com/2012/11/05/what-president-obama-really-said-60-minutes-interview-about-benghazi [Retrieved April 16, 2013].

Barnes, A.M. (1999) "Competency, coercion, and risk of violence: legal intersects with fundamental issues of mental health", *Marquette Law Review*, 82: 713-22.

Benford, R.D. and Hunt, S.A. (2003) "Interactional dynamics in public problems marketplaces: movements and the counterframing and reframing of public problems", in (eds) *Challenges and choices: Constructionist perspectives on social problems*, Hawthorne, NY: Aldine de Gruyter, pp 153-86.

Benford, R.D. and Snow, D.A. (2000) "Framing processes and social movements: an overview and assessment", *Annual Review of Sociology*, 26: 611-39.

Benshoff, H.M. and Griffin, S. (2006) *Queer images: A history of gay and lesbian film in America*, Lanham, MD: Rowman & Littlefield.

Best, J. (1990) *Threatened children: Rhetoric and concern about child-victims*, Chicago, IL: University of Chicago Press.

Best, J. (1999) *Random violence*, Berkeley, CA: University of California Press.

Best, J. (2008) *Social problems*, New York, NY: W.W. Norton and Company.

Best, J. (2013) *Social problems* (2nd edn), New York: W.W. Norton and Company.

Best, J. (2015) "Halloween sadism: the evidence", Newark, DE: University of Delaware. Available at: http://www.udel.edu/soc/faculty/best/site/halloween.html#article [Retrieved January 28, 2015].

Best, J. and Horiuchi, G.T. (1985) "The razor blade in the apple: the social construction of urban legends", *Social Problems*, 32: 488-99.

Binder, A. (1993) "Constructing racial rhetoric: media depictions of harm in heavy metal and rap music", *American Sociological Review*, 48: 753-67.

Bloom, M. (2012) "Tragic but rare: odds of dying in a school shooting, as in Chardon, about one in a million", *National Public Radio*, February 27. Available at: https://stateimpact.npr.org/ohio/2012/02/27/tragic-but-rare-odds-of-dying-in-a-school-shooting-as-in-chardon-at-least-one-in-a-million/ [Retrieved August 22, 2015].

Blumer, H. (1971) "Social problems as collective behavior", *Social Problems*, 18: 298-306.

Breast Cancer Action (2016) "Think before you pink", Available at: http://thinkbeforeyoupink.org/before-you-buy/ [Retrieved January 8, 2016]

British Broadcasting Corporation (BBC) (2014) "From 'Modern Family' to 'Glee': how TV advanced gay rights", September 24. Available at: http://www.bbc.com/culture/story/20140924-the-biggest-ally-of-gay-rights [Retrieved December 16, 2015].

Brown, W.J. (2003) "The influence of famous athletes on health beliefs and practices: Mark McGwire, child abuse prevention, and androstenedione", *Journal of Health Communication*, 8: 41-57.

Brubaker, J. (2008) "Best supporting actor: the third-person effect of celebrity political endorsements", *Ohio Communication Journal*, 46: 1-13.

Callanan, V.J. (2012) "Media consumption, perceptions of crime risk and fear of crime: examining race/ethnic differences", *Sociological Perspectives*, 55: 93-115.

Carlson, D.K. (2002) The Blame Game: Youth and Media Violence", Washington DC: Gallup. Available at: http://www.gallup.com/poll/5626/blame-game-youth-media-violence.aspx [Retrieved January 26, 2015].

CBS News (2010) "McConnell: WikiLeaks head a high-tech terrorist", December 5. Available at: http://www.cbsnews.com/2100-501707_162-7119787.html [Retrieved February 22, 2013].

The Center for Media and Public Affairs (2012) *Study: Media framed Benghazi in Obama's terms*, Arlington, VA: The Center for Media and Public Affairs. Available at: http://www.cmpa.com/media_room_press_05_13_13.html [Retrieved April 18, 2013].

Chandler, C. (2014) "Hollywood's immoral agenda", April 2. Available at: http://billygraham.org/decision-magazine/april-2014/hollywoods-immoral-agenda/ [Retrieved July 23, 2014].

Chokshi, N. (2016a) "Rudy Giuliani: Beyoncé's halftime show was an 'outrageous' affront to police", *The Washington Post*, February 8. Available at: https://www.washingtonpost.com/news/arts-and-entertainment/wp/2016/02/08/rudy-giuliani-beyonces-half-time-show-was-an-outrageous-affront-to-police/ [Retrieved March 28, 2016].

Chokshi, N. (2016b) "Sheriffs: Beyoncé is 'inciting bad behavior' and endangering law enforcement", *The Washington Post*, February 18. Available at: https://www.washingtonpost.com/news/post-nation/wp/2016/02/18/the-beyonce-backlash-continues-sheriff-cites-super-bowl-show-after-shooting-near-home/ [Retrieved March 28, 2016].

CNN (2013) "Sources: possible suspects sought in Boston blasts", April 17. Available at: http://news.blogs.cnn.com/2013/04/17/source-arrest-made-in-boston-bombing/ [Retrieved April 24, 2013].

Cohen, S. (2002) *Folk devils and moral panics: The creation of the mods and rockers* (3rd edn), New York, NY: Routledge.

Cohen, A.P., Azrael, D. and Miller, M. (2014) "Rate of mass shootings has tripled since 2011, Harvard research shows", *Mother Jones*, October 15. Available at: http://www.motherjones.com/politics/2014/10/mass-shootings-increasing-harvard-research [Retrieved September 1, 2015.

Combs, J. (1984) *Polpop: Politics and popular culture in America*, Bowling Green, OH: Bowling Green University Popular Press.

Curry, T. (2012) "NRA blames media, music and more for culture of violence", *NBC News*, December 21. Available at: http://nbcpolitics.nbcnews.com/_news/2012/12/21/16069537-nra-blames-media-music-and-more-for-culture-of-violence [Retrieved January 24, 2015].

Davis, H.P. (1974) "The early history of broadcasting in the United States", in *The radio industry: The story of its development*, New York: Arno Press, pp 189-225.

Debord, G-E. and Wolman, G.J. (1956) "Mode d'emploi du détournement", *Les lèvres nues*, 8. Available at: http://sami.is.free. fr/Oeuvres/debord_wolman_mode_emploi_detournement.html [Retrieved January 12, 2016].

De Fleur, M.L. (1966) *Theories of mass communication*, New York: David McKay.

Deutsch, S.K. and Gray Cavender (2008) "CSI and forensic realism", *Journal of Criminal Justice and Popular Culture*, 15: 34–53.

Dewey, C. (2014) "The complete, terrifying history of 'Slender Man,' the internet meme that compelled two 12-year olds to stab their friend", *The Washington Post*, June 3. Available at: https://www.washingtonpost. com/news/the-intersect/wp/2014/06/03/the-complete-terrifying-history-of-slender-man-the-internet-meme-that-compelled-two-12-year-olds-to-stab-their-friend/ [Retrieved April 20, 2016].

Diamond, J. (2015) "Tom Brady: I wasn't endorsing Donald Trump", *CNN*, September 29. Available at: http://www.cnn.com/2015/09/29/ politics/tom-brady-not-endorsing-donald-trump/ [Retrieved December 15, 2015].

DiMaggio, P., Hargittai, E., Russell Neuman, W. and Robinson, J.P. (2001) "Social implications of the internet", *Annual Review of Sociology*, 27: 307–36.

Dittmer, J. (2012) *Captain America and the nationalist superhero: Metaphors, narratives, and geopolitics*, Philadelphia, PA: Temple University Press.

Doyle, A. (2003) *Arresting images: Crime and policing in front of the television camera*, Toronto: University of Toronto Press.

Drash, W. (2009) "'Horrorcore' singer suspected in Virginia killings", *CNN*, October 6. Available at: http://www.cnn.com/2009/ CRIME/10/06/virginia.horrorcore.killings/ [Retrieved February 18, 2015].

Eggerton, J. (2013) "Rockefeller introduces violence research bill", *Broadcasting & Cable*, March 4. Available at: http://www. broadcastingcable.com/news/washington/poll-most-americans-believe-media-violence-contributes-real-violence/61170 [Retrieved January 24, 2015].

Emery, E., Ault P.H. and Agee, W.K. (1973) *Introduction to mass communications*, New York, NY: Dodd, Mead & Company.

Endersby, J.W. and Towle, M.J. (1996) "Tailgate partisanship: political and social expression through bumper stickers", *Social Science Journal*, 33: 307–19.

Farley, C.J. (1999) "Hip-Hop Nation", *Time*, February 4. Available at: http://content.time.com/time/magazine/article/0,9171,19134,00. html [Retrieved December 23, 2015].

Fedorak, S.A. (2009) *Pop Culture: The culture of everyday life*, Toronto: University of Toronto Press.

Fernandez, S.M. (1998) "Pretty in Pink: The life and times of the ribbon that tied breast cancer to corporate giving", *MAMM,* (June/ July). Available at: http://thinkbeforeyoupink.org/before-you-buy/ history-of-the-pink-ribbon/ [Retrieved January 8, 2016].

Fishman, M. (1980) *Manufacturing the news*, Austin, TX: University of Texas Press.

Fiske, J. (1995) "Popular culture", in F. Lentricchia and T. McLaughlin (eds) *Critical terms for literary study* (2nd edn), Chicago, IL: The University of Chicago Press, pp 321-35.

Fiske, J. (2010) *Understanding popular culture* (2nd edn), New York, NY: Routledge.

Follman, M., Aronsen, G. and Pan, D. (2012) "A guide to mass shootings in America", *Mother Jones*, July 20. Available at: http://www. motherjones.com/politics/2012/07/mass-shootings-map [Retrieved March 22, 2013].

Fox, J.A. (2013) "Mass shootings not trending", *Boston.com*, January 23. Available at: http://www.boston.com/community/blogs/crime_ punishment/2013/01/mass_shootings_not_trending.html [Retrieved September 1, 2015].

Fox, R.L., Van Sickel, R.W. and Steiger, T.L. (2007) *Tabloid justice: Criminal justice in an age of media frenzy* (2nd edn), Boulder, CO: Lynne Rienner.

Freedman, J.L. (2002) *Media violence and its effect on aggression: Assessing the scientific evidence.* Toronto: University of Toronto Press.

Friedman, E. (2010) "BP Buys 'oil' search terms to redirect users to official company website", *ABC News*, June 5. Available at: http:// abcnews.go.com/Technology/bp-buys-search-engine-phrases- redirecting-users/story?id=10835618 [Retrieved January 2, 2013].

Frost, C. (2008) "The other man on the podium", *BBC*, October 17. Available at: http://news.bbc.co.uk/2/hi/uk_news/magazine/7674157. stm [Retrieved January 12, 2016].

Gainor, D. (2013) "Liberal media spin Benghazi scandal to protect team Obama", *Fox News*, May 9. Available at: http://www.foxnews.com/ opinion/2013/05/09/liberal-media-spin-benghazi-scandal-to-protect- team-obama/ [Retrieved May 12, 2013].

Gallo, C. (2014) "How Pete Frates found his calling and launched the ice bucket challenge", *Forbes*, September 5. Available at: http://www.forbes.com/sites/carminegallo//09/05/how-pete-frates-found-his-calling-and-launched-the-ice-bucket-challenge/ [Retrieved September 20, 2015].

Gallup (2016) *Gay and lesbian rights*, Washington D.C.: Gallup. Available at: http://www.gallup.com/poll/1651/gay-lesbian-rights.aspx [Retrieved February 22, 2016].

Gamson, W.A., Croteau, D., Hoynes, W. and Sasson, T. (1992) "Media images and the social construction of reality", *Annual Review of Sociology*, 18: 373-93.

Garcia, A. (2016) "Georgia, N.C. and beyond: what you need to know about the clash over 'anti-gay' bills", *CNN*, March 26. Available at: http://money.cnn.com/2016/03/26/news/anti-lgbt-bills-north-carolina-georgia/ [Retrieved March 28, 2016].

Gitlin, T. (1980) *The whole world is watching*, Berkeley, CA: University of California Press.

GLAAD (2015) "2015-16 where we are on TV", Los Angeles, CA: GLAAD. Available at: http://www.glaad.org/whereweareontv15 [Retrieved December 16, 2015].

Glassner, B. (1999) *The culture of fear*, New York, NY: Basic Books.

Glasspiegel, R. (2013) "PETA photoshopped a bleeding rat into the NFL logo to protest animal cruelty", *Sports Illustrated*, September 12. Available at: http://www.si.com/extra-mustard/2013/09/12/nfl-animal-cruelty-testing-peta [Retrieved March 10, 2016].

Graber, D.A. (1988) *Processing the news*, White Plains, NY: Longman.

Gramsci, A. (1971) [Q. Hoare and G.N. Smith (eds)] *Selections from the prison notebooks*, New York, NY: International Publishers.

Granovetter, M.S. (1973) "The strength of weak ties", *American Journal of Sociology*, 78: 1360-80.

Grazian, D. (2010) *Mix it up? Popular culture, mass media, and society*, New York, NY: W.W. Norton & Company.

Grinberg, E. (2012) "Hasbro to unveil black and silver Easy-Bake Oven after teen's petition", *CNN*, December 18. Available at: http://www.cnn.com/2012/12/18/living/hasbro-easy-bake-oven [Retrieved April 3, 2013].

Gross, L. and Woods, J.D. (1999) "Introduction: being gay in American media and society", in L. Gross and J.D. Woods (eds) *The Columbia reader: On lesbians and gay men in media, society, and politics*, New York, NY: Columbia University Press, pp 3-22.

Haberman, C. (2016) "When Dungeons & Dragons set off a 'moral panic'", *The New York Times*, April 17. Available at: http://www.nytimes.com/2016/04/18/us/when-dungeons-dragons-set-off-a-moral-panic.html [Retrieved April 18, 2016].

Hilgartner, S. and Bosk, C.L. (1988) "The rise and fall of social problems: a public arenas model", *The American Journal of Sociology*, 94: 53-78.

Horkheimer, M. and Adorno, T.W. [1944] (2002) [G.S. Noerr (ed) E. Jephcott (trans)] *Dialectic of enlightenment: Philosophical fragments*, Stanford, CA: Stanford University Press.

Horovitz, B. (2014) "Burger King sells gay pride Whopper", *USA Today*, July 1. Available at: http://www.usatoday.com/story/money/business/2014/07/01/burger-king-gay-pride-burger-parade-fast-food-gay-rights/11903861/ [Retrieved April 2, 2016].

Isidore, C. (2015) "'Paid patriotism' at NFL games blasted in Senate report", *CNN*, November 4. Available at: http://money.cnn.com/2015/11/04/news/companies/team-paid-military-tributes/ [Retrieved January 4, 2016].

Jenness, V. 919950 "Social movement growth, domain expansion, and framing processes: the gay/lesbian movement and violence against gays and lesbians as a social problem", *Social Problems*, 42: 145-70.

Jones, R.H. (2015) "Generic intertextuality in online social activism: the case of the It Gets Better Project", *Language in Society*, 44: 317-39.

Kavanaugh, P.R. and Maratea, R.J (2014) "[A]moral panics and risk in contemporary drug and viral pandemic claims", in T.L. Anderson (ed) *Understanding Deviance: Connecting classical and contemporary perspectives*, New York: Routledge, pp 378-88.

Kellinger, J.J.and Levine, L. (2016) "While you wait: an analysis of the It Gets Better Project", *Queer Studies in Media & Popular Culture*, 1: 85-94.

Kepple, K.A., Loehrke, J., Hoyer, M. and Overberg, P. (2013) "Mass shootings toll exceeds 900 in past seven years", *USA Today*, December 2. Available at: http://www.usatoday.com/story/news/nation/2013/02/21/mass-shootings-domestic-violence-nra/1937041/ [Retrieved September 1, 2015].

Kidd, D. (2014) *Pop Culture Freaks: Identity, mass media and society*, Boulder, CO: Westview Press.

King, S. (2008) *Pink Ribbons, Inc.: Breast cancer and the politics of philanthropy*, Minneapolis, MN: University of Minnesota Press.

King, S. (2010) "Pink Ribbons Inc.: the emergence of cause-related marketing and the corporatization of the breast cancer movement", in *Governing the Female Body: Gender, health, and networks of power*, Albany, NY: SUNY Press, pp 85-111.

Klapp, O.E. (1964) *Symbolic Leaders: Public dramas and public men*. London: Minerva Press.

Kornhaber, S. (2015) "The 'Modern Family' effect: pop culture's role in the gay-marriage revolution", *The Atlantic*, June 26. Available at: http://www.theatlantic.com/entertainment/archive/2015/06/gay-marriage-legalized-modern-family-pop-culture/397013/ [Retrieved December 16, 2015].

Kort-Butler, L.A. and Sittner Hartshorn, K.J. (2011) "Watching the detectives: crime programming, fear of crime, and attitudes about the criminal justice system", *The Sociological Quarterly*, 52: 36-55.

LaCapria, K. (2015) "Fright night bite", *Snopes.com*, October 25. Available at: http://www.snopes.com/fright-night-bite/ [Retrieved October 29, 2015].

Lett, P. (2015) "Jon Stewart's legacy", *The New York Times*, August 7. Available at: http://takingnote.blogs.nytimes.com/2015/08/07/jon-stewarts-legacy/ [Retrieved August 11, 2015].

Lewin, T. (2012) "Black students face more discipline, data suggests", *The New York Times*, March 6. Available at: http://www.newyorktimes.com/2012/03/06/education/black-students-face-more-harsh-discipline-data-shows.html [Retrieved April 1, 2014].

Lilley, T.G., Best, J., Aguirre, B.E.and Lowney, K.S. (2010) "Magnetic imagery: War-related ribbons as collective display", *Sociological Inquiry*, 80: 313-21.

Loseke, D.R. (2003) "Constructing conditions, people, morality, and emotion: expanding the agenda of constructionism", in J.A. Holstein and G. Miller (eds) *Challenges & Choices: Constructionist perspectives on social problems*, Hawthorne, NY: Aldine de Gruyter, pp 120-29.

MacAskill, E. (2010) "Julian Assange like a hi-tech terrorist, says Joe Biden", *The Guardian*, December 19. Available at: http://www.guardian .co.uk/media/2010/dec/19/assange-high-tech-terrorist-biden [Retrieved February 24, 2013].

Mandel, S. (2014) "Michael Sam breaks longstanding barrier by announcing he is gay", *Sports Illustrated*, February 10. Available at: http://www.si.com/nfl/2014/02/10/michael-sam-missouri-tigers-nfl-draft [Retrieved December 1, 2015].

Manjoo, F. (2006) "The 9/11 deniers", *Salon*, June 27. Available at: http://www.salon.com/2006/06/27/911_conspiracies/ [Retrieved April 1, 2016].

Manjoo, F. (2008) *True enough: Learning to live in a post-fact society*, Hoboken, NJ: Wiley.

Maratea, R.J. (2014) *The politics of the internet: Political claims-making in cyberspace and how it's affecting modern political activism*, Lanham, MD: Lexington.

Maratea, R.J. and Monahan, B.A. (2013) "Crime control as mediated spectacle: the institutionalization of gonzo rhetoric in modern media and politics", *Symbolic Interaction*, 36: 261-74.

Marcuse, H. [1964] (1991) *One-dimensional man: Studies in the ideology of advanced industrial society*, Boston, MA: Beacon Press.

Martinez, E. (2009) ""Syko" Sam's alleged victims remembered, suspect was horrorcore rapper", *CBS News*, October 6. Available at: http://www.cbsnews.com/news/syko-sams-alleged-victims-remembered-suspect-was-horrorcore-rapper/ [Retrieved February 20, 2015].

McCarthy, J.D. and Zald, M.N. (1977) "Resource mobilization and social movements: a partial theory", *American Journal of Sociology* 82: 1212-41.

Meyer, D.S. and Gamson, J. (1995) "The challenge of cultural elites: celebrities and social movements, *Sociological Inquiry*, 65:181-206.

Meyrowitz, J. (1994) "Medium theory", in *Communication theory today*, Stanford, CA: Stanford University Press, pp 50-77.

Michaud, J. (2015) "The tangled cultural roots of Dungeons & Dragons", *The New Yorker*, November 2. Available at: http://www.newyorker.com/books/page-turner/the-tangled-cultural-roots-of-dungeons-dragons [Retrieved April 18, 2016].

Monahan, B.A. (2010) *The shock of the news: Media coverage and the making of 9/11*, New York, NY: NYU Press.

Monahan, J., Steadman, H.J., Robbins, P.C., Appelbaum, P., Banks, S., Grisso, T., Heilbrun, K., Mulvey, E.P., Roth, L. and Silver, E. (2005) "An actuarial model of violence risk assessment for persons with mental disorders", *Psychiatric Services*, 56: 810-15.

Moore, K., Stuewig, J. and Tangney, J. (2013) "Jail inmates' perceived and anticipated stigma: implications for post-release functioning", *Self Identify*, 12: 527-47.

Murashko, A. (2014) "Burger King's limited edition gay pride Whopper may go national, promotes homosexual behavior as healthy, warns AFA", *The Christian Post*, July 17. Available at: http://www.christianpost.com/news/burger-kings-limited-edition-gay-pride-whopper-may-go-national-promotes-homosexual-behavior-as-healthy-warns-afa-123420/ [Retrieved April 2, 2016]

Nagarajan, C. (2015) "#Bringbackourgirls hasn't brought back Chibok's girls, but it has changed Nigeria's politics", *The Guardian*, April 14. Available at: http://www.theguardian.com/commentisfree/2015/apr/14/nigeria-women-activists-boko-haram [Retrieved April 13, 2016].

National Football League (2016) "A crucial catch: annual screenings saves lives", *NFL.com*. Available at: http://www.nfl.com/pink [Retrieved January 5, 2016].

National Public Radio (2010) "Are charities doing enough to fight breast cancer?", October 25. Available at: http://www.npr.org/templates/story/story.php?storyId=130810038 [Retrieved January 2, 2016].

NBC News (2012) "Biden breaks down stance on same-sex marriage", *Meet the Press*, May 6. New York, NY: National Broadcasting Company. Available at: http://www.nbcnews.com/video/meet-the-press/47312632#47312632 [Retrieved December 12, 2015].

Nip, J.Y.M. (2004) "The queer sisters and its electronic bulletin board: a study of the internet for social movement mobilization", *Information, Communication & Society*, 7: 23-49.

Notte, J. (2015) "Opinion: the NFL's pink October is a publicity stunt", *Marketwatch*, October 21. Available at: http://www.marketwatch.com/story/the-nfls-pink-october-is-a-publicity-stunt-2015-10-21 [Retrieved January 6, 2015].

Nussbaum, E. (2014) "The great divide: Norman Lear, Archie Bunker, and the rise of the bad fan", *The New Yorker*, April 7. Available at: http://www.newyorker.com/magazine/2014/04/07/the-great-divide-emily-nussbaum [Retrieved April 22, 2016].

Payton, J.W., Wardlaw, D.M., Graczyk, P.A., Bloodworth, M.R., Tompsett, C.J. and Weissberg, R.P. (2000) "Social and emotional learning: a framework for promoting mental health and reducing risk behavior in children and youth", *Journal of School Health*, 70: 179-85.

Perez, V.W. (2013) "The Movement linking vaccines to autism: parents and the internet", in J. Best and S.R. Harris (eds) *New images, new issues: Making sense of social problems*,. Boulder, CO: Lynne Rienner, pp 71-89.

Peralta, E. (2015) "Pentagon paid sports teams millions for 'paid patriotism' events", *National Public Radio*, November 5. Available at: http://www.npr.org/sections/thetwo-way/2015/11/05/454834662/pentagon-paid-sports-teams-millions-for-paid-patriotism-events [Retrieved January 6, 2016]

Petersilia, J. (2000) "When prisoners return to the community: political, economic, and social consequences", *Sentencing & Corrections: Issues for the 21st Century*, November. Washington D.C.: National Institute of Justice, US Department of Justice.

Pew Research Center (2013) *Benghazi investigation does not reignite broad public interest*, Washington D.C.: Pew Research Center for the People & the Press, Pew Research Center. Available at: http://www.people-press.org/2013/05/13/benghazi-investigation-does-not-reignite-broad-public-interest/ [Retrieved April 15, 2013].

Pew Research Center (2015) "Support for same-sex marriage at record high, but key segments remain opposed: 72% say legal recognition is inevitable", Washington, D.C.: Pew Research Center. Available at: http://www.people-press.org/2015/06/08/support-for-same-sex-marriage-at-record-high-but-key-segments-remain-opposed/ [Retrieved December 21, 2015].

Phillips, N.D. and Strobl, S. (2013) *Comic book crime: Truth, justice, and the American way*, New York: NYU Press.

Postman, N. (1985) *Amusing ourselves to death: Public discourse in the age of show business*, New York: Viking Penguin.

Rafter, N. (2006) *Shots in the mirror: Crime films and society* (2nd edn), New York: Oxford University Press.

Raley, A.B. and Lucas, J.L. (2006) "Prime-time television's portrayals of gay male, lesbian, and bisexual characters", *Journal of Homosexuality*, 51(2):19-38.

Rapoza, K. (2011) "Fox News viewers uninformed, NPR listeners not, poll suggests", *Forbes*, November 21. Available at: http://www.forbes.com/sites/kenrapoza/2011/11/21/fox-news-viewers-uninformed-npr-listeners-not-poll-suggests/ [Retrieved May 29, 2013].

Rasmussen Reports (2012) "52% say violence in video games, movies leads to more violence in society." Asbury Park, NJ.: Rasmussen Reports. Available at: http://www.rasmussenreports.com/public_content/lifestyle/general_lifestyle/july_2012/52_say_violence_in_video_games_movies_leads_to_more_violence_in_society [Retrieved January 24, 2015].

Rattan, A. and Ambady, N. (2014) "How 'It Gets Better': effectively communicating support to targets of prejudice", *Personality and Social Psychology Bulletin*, 40: 555-566.

Reagan, R. (1981) "Remarks at the Annual Meeting of the National Alliance of Business", Presented at the Annual Meeting of the National Alliance of Business, October 5, Washington D.C. Available at: http://www.reagan.utexas.edu/archives/speeches/1981/100581a.htm [Retrieved December 29, 2015].

Ritz, E. (2014) "The conversation Glenn Beck is begging Americans to have in the wake of the Santa Barbara killing spree", *The Blaze*, May 27. Available at: http://www.theblaze.com/stories/2014/05/27/the-conversation-glenn-beck-is-begging-americans-to-have-in-the-wake-of-the-santa-barbara-killing-spree/ [Retrieved August 15, 2015].

Rowe, D. (1995) *Popular cultures: Rock music, sport, and the politics of pleasure*, Thousand Oaks, CA: Sage.

Ruibal, S. (2007) "Armstrong wristbands yield $63 million to fight cancer", *USA Today*, July 17. Available at: http://usatoday30.usatoday.com/sports/cycling/tourdefrance/2007-07-16-Armstrong-wristbands_N.htm [Retrieved January 4, 2016].

Russo, V. (1987) *The Celluloid Closet: Homosexuality in the movies* (revised edn), New York, NY: Harper & Row.

Sacco, V.F. (2005) *When crime waves*, Thousand Oaks, CA: Sage Publications.

Sales, N.J. (2015) "Tinder and the dawn of the 'dating apocalypse'", *Vanity Fair*, August 6. Available at: http://www.vanityfair.com/culture/2015/08/tinder-hook-up-culture-end-of-dating [Retrieved August 11, 2015].

San Jose Mercury News (2012) "Transcript: National Rifle Association press conference advocating armed guards in American schools", , December 21. Available at: http://www.mercurynews.com/california/ci_22241206/transcript-national-rifle-association-press-conference-advocating-armed [Retrieved August 15, 2015].

Santino, J. (1992) "Yellow ribbons and seasonal flags: the folk assemblage of war", *The Journal of American Folklore*, 105(415): 19-33.

Savage, D. and Miller, T. (eds) (2011) *It gets better: Coming out, overcoming bullying, and creating a life worth living*, New York, NY: Dutton.

Self, J. (2014) "How proud is the proud Whopper?", *The Advocate*, September 1. Available at: http://www.advocate.com/print-issue/current-issue/2014/09/01/how-proud-proud-whopper [Retrieved April 2, 2016]

Sellnow, D.D. (2014) *The rhetorical power of popular culture: Considering mediated texts* (2nd edn), Thousand Oaks, CA: Sage.

Sherwell, P. (2014) "Father of 'virgin killer' Elliot Rodger: 'none of us understood what was in his head'", *The Telegraph*, June 27. Available at: http://www.telegraph.co.uk/news/worldnews/northamerica/usa/10930847/Father-of-virgin-killer-Elliot-Rodger-None-of-us-understood-what-was-in-his-head.html [Retrieved September 3, 2015].

Siddique, H. and Weaver, M. (2010) "US Embassy cables culprit should be executed, says Mike Huckabee", *The Guardian*, December 1. Available at: http://www.guardian.co.uk/world/2010/dec/01/us-embassy-cables-executed-mike-huckabee [Retrieved February 24, 2013].

Sinha, S. (2014) "The NFL's pink October does not raise money for cancer research", *Vice Sports*, October 8. Available at: https://sports.vice.com/en_us/article/the-nfls-pink-october-does-not-raise-money-for-cancer-research [Retrieved January 6, 2016].

Smith, H. (1988) "Badges, buttons, t-shirts and bumperstickers: the semiotics of some recursive systems", *Journal of Popular Culture*, 21: 141-49.

Snow, D.A., Rochford Jr., E.B., Worden, S.K. and Benford, R.D. (1986) "Frame alignment processes, micromobilization, and movement participation", *American Sociological Review*, 51: 464-81.

Snow, R.P. (1983) *Creating media culture*, Beverly Hills, CA: Sage.

Spector, M. and Kitsuse, J.I. (1987) *Constructing social problems*, Hawthorne, NY: Aldine de Gruyter.

Steinberg, N. (2013) "Mass shootings not a big problem", *Chicago Sun-Times*, April 4. Available at: http://www.suntimes.com/news/steinberg/19270756-452/mass-shootings-not-a-big-problem.html [Retrieved April 7, 2013].

Steinmetz, K. (2014) "Burger King debuts gay pride Whopper", *Time*, July 1. Available at: http://time.com/2947156/burger-king-debuts-gay-pride-whopper/ [Retrieved April 2, 2016].

Street, J. (2002) "Bob, Bono and Tony B: the popular artist as politician", *Media, Culture & Society*, 24: 433-41.

Swanson, E. (2014) "There's still a lot of work to be done for pit bulls, poll finds", *Huffington Post*, July 29. Available at: http://www.huffingtonpost.com/2014/07/29/pit-bulls-poll_n_5628261.html [Retrieved January 5, 2016].

Takacs, S. (2012) *Terrorism TV: Popular entertainment in post-9/11 America*, Lawrence, KS: University Press of Kansas.

Trend, D. (2007) *The myth of media violence: A critical introduction*, Malden, MA: Blackwell Publishing.

US Senate (1954a) Interim report of the Committee on the Judiciary, *Comic books and juvenile delinquency: Interim report,* 84th Cong, 1st sess, pp 23-32.

US Senate (1954b) Senate Subcommittee to Investigate Juvenile Delinquency of the Committee on the Judiciary, *Juvenile delinquency (comic books): Hearing,* 83rd Cong, 2nd sess.

Ungar, S. (1992) "The rise and (relative) decline of global warming as a social problem", *The Sociological Quarterly*, 33: 483-501.

Useem, B. and Zald, M.N. (1982) "Pressure groups to social movement: organizational dilemmas of the effort to promote nuclear power", *Social Problems*, 30: 144-56.

van Dijk, T.A. (1996) "Power and the news media", in D.L. Paletz (ed) *Political Communication and Action*, Cresskill, NJ: Hampton Press, pp 9-36.

Wemple, E. (2013) "CNN's double breakdown: so much for 'abundance of caution'", *The Washington Post*, April 17. Available at: http://www.washingtonpost.com/blogs/erik-wemple/wp/2013/04/17/boston-bombing-suspect-cnn-double-breakdown-so-much-for-abundance-of-caution/ [Retrieved April 18, 2013].

Wertham, F. (1954) *Seduction of the innocent*, New York, NY: Rinehart.

Whalen, J. and Crawford, D. (2010) "How WikiLeaks keeps its funding secret", *The Wall Street Journal*, August 23. Available at: http://online.wsj.com/article/SB10001424052748704554104575436231926853198.html [Retrieved February 21, 2013].

Zelizer, V.A. (1994) *Pricing the priceless child: The changing social value of children*, Princeton, NJ: Princeton University Press.

Index

Lightning Source UK Ltd.
Milton Keynes UK
UKHW031023141118
332321UK00005B/256/P